About the Authors:

BONNIE B. JUROE is a graduate of Santa Ana College, where she was honored as one of the "Women of the Year." Mrs. Juroe is currently pursuing a counseling degree and serves on the Women's Ministries Council in her church.

DAVID J. JUROE is a full-time practicing marriage, family, and child counselor at the Yorba Park Medical Clinic and an affiliate staff member of the Chapman General Hospital, both in Orange, California. He holds a Ph.D. in psychology, has been ordained as a minister, and has recently been elected to Who's Who in California. Dr. Juroe has taught on college and seminary levels, and has written and edited a number of books, including *Money*. He conducts seminars with his wife on the subject of step-families and related topics. Their blended family includes eight children, three of whom live with them in Orange, California.

SUCCESSFUL STEPPARENTING

SUCCESSFUL STEPPARENTING

David J. and Bonnie B. Juroe

977

Fleming H. Revell Company
Old Tappan, New Jersey

Library of Congress Cataloging in Publication Data

Juroe, David J.
    Successful stepparenting.

    Bibliography: p.
    Includes index.
    1. Stepparents.   2. Parenting.   3. Stepchildren.
    4. Children of divorced parents.   I. Juroe, Bonnie B.
    II. Title.
    HQ759.92.J87   1983   646.7′8   82-20449
    ISBN 0-8007-1339-7

With deepest love and grateful appreciation we dedicate this book to each other, because we have found in each other mutual trust, respect, and support. These cherished gifts have created a refuge of acceptance, encouragement, fulfillment, and joy, upholding us in the rebuilding of our lives.

We further dedicate this book to our eight children. They meaningfully contributed toward the awareness of the real issues, the significance of affiliation, and the importance of the honesty, integrity, and cooperation required to sustain successful relationships in our stepfamily.

His	*Hers*	*Ours*
James	Wendy	Davonna
Judith	Christina	
Janice		
Julia		
Jonathan		

Contents

Preface

Each year there are a million new stepchildren in America. There is no question that trying to blend broken families may possibly be the most serious and complex social and mental health crisis affecting children in the eighties. And, in spite of the comforting old view that children have a remarkable way of "bouncing back," evidence points to the fact that trauma and deep hurt are experienced by many stepchildren who may not recover for years.

We, ourselves, entered into remarriage with high hopes and enthusiasm and became stepparents as Bonnie brought her two children and David brought his five into our new stepfamily. Little did we realize that we walked into a world vastly different from what we expected.

Strange, we had the notion that our family would be different. We thought we could rise above any problem. After all, we had the Lord. We felt mature and ready to take on the task of salving the pain of family breakup. Then, too, as counselors we do have some understanding about people, their emotions, and their interpersonal relationships. We thought this would totally qualify us to achieve great success.

It was not long after our wedding that we began to notice certain behavior patterns and responses in our children that puzzled us very much. We began to sense rejection, confusion, isolation, and frustration for which we really had no explanation. The discovery was shocking. We found few role models, and professional counselors were mainly in the dark, too, about how to be successful stepparents. You could count on one hand the books available on the subject.

Children entering a stepfamily can feel twice defeated, once for having been unable to prevent the breakup of their parents and again for not being able to prevent the remarriage. Shock, followed by depression, anger, and denial, and decreasingly low self-esteem—such intense reverberations influence every aspect of a stepchild's life, to say nothing about the parents in the new family.

The aftermath can be a maze of confusion and conflict. For some children this never is resolved. Others may get through it with few scars if they were fortunate enough to grow up in a healthy stepfamily. Family-counseling professionals call them "survivors," because they become more self-reliant, better adjusted, and more relaxed because of the removal of tension they felt in their original family.

After our remarriage stepparents seemed to come from everywhere. The discovery was heartwarming, for we came to realize that we were really not alone. As we began to talk and relate to others in stepfamilies, we found that they, too, experienced much frustration and disappointment.

Other parents began turning to us for help. We began by starting a monthly support group in our home, sponsored by our church. For want of a better term, we called it a "reconstituted family" support group. Our little group was small, but how we related to each other! The demand became greater as other church groups extended invitations for us to lead seminars on the subject. YMCAs and civic clubs joined in.

This book, then, is the result of personal experience and has grown out of hundreds of counseling hours, on a professional level, with individuals who have in some way been associated with the severe problems found in most stepfamilies. The tremendous needs and hurts shared by many people made us very aware of the need for a book of this kind.

This issue of stepfamilies is far more than a passing subject in our fractured, topsy-turvy world. It is an immensely compelling topic. Divorce has become epidemic in our Western world. The subject therefore cannot be ignored.

We not only wish directly to help stepparents and those who may be close to them, but we have another distinct purpose in writing this book. We'd like to speak gently but persuasively to the church of our generation. We all know there are judgmental groups in many denominations who look askance at divorced and remarried people as well as those who are stepparents. Our interest mainly lies in taking a closer look at the problems. They exist and we hope that many will see the tremendous needs and will rally to support the person who has hurts with which few can really identify unless they have experienced them themselves.

Ours is not to argue over the rightness or wrongness of divorce or remarriage. There are available today some fine new books by very able authors that discuss this issue. We just want to deal with the stepfamily problems realistically and helpfully. We have to remember that, as a part of God's plan, it is not for us to judge but to minister to the hurting. The question now is not *if* we will reach out but *how* is the best way to support these hurting individuals.

We do ardently believe that many segments of the Christian world that were perhaps once afraid to touch this subject are now ready. We used to hear from many quarters: "After all, if you talk about remarriage problems, aren't you condoning divorce?" Others may have believed that all divorced people are losers, and surely they didn't want to be around such failures—it might rub off on them. Because the increase of divorce and remarriage is a major social problem in our society and churches, the sticky subject of stepfamilies must be met head-on. We can't afford any head-in-the-sand approaches. If you get nothing out of this book other than a newer realization that stepfamilies have special hurts and stand in need of genuine concern and support, we will have accomplished our goal.

As counselors, we have come to see the great importance of reaching out redemptively to a growing segment of our population. There is a great rise in the number of people waiting for help because of the staggering problems encountered in stepfamilies. Many parents really do care about their children's needs. They do sincerely want to help them through the pain of a divorce or remarriage, but many do not know how or where to begin because they do not really understand what is going on. We are convinced that if more people are familiar with the reasons behind the stresses they have to cope with, the quality and durability of their new relationships would be greatly enhanced. Those contemplating remarriage where children are involved need to have insight as well as courage to come to a decision.

We have not tried to do the impossible, that is, to consider in depth every conceivable problem encountered in the stepfamily. To do so would require volumes. Rather, we have chosen to narrow our subject matter so as not to simply rehash but to add to the field of knowledge by examining deeper levels that have not as yet been extensively explored. We are quite aware that there are some reasonably happy stepfamilies. We know some individuals who have come through beautifully, who may thank God every day for a caring and loving stepparent. Some children do seem to approve of and look forward to their parent's remarrying, especially when there has been a lot of discord in their original home. This book has not been written so much for them as for the stepfamily in trouble—one that may need to be lifted out of despair and disillusionment.

In a book of this kind one is inevitably using and building on the accumulated wisdom of many people. We sincerely and gratefully acknowledge our debt to them.

Basically, however, this work represents an extension of ourselves born out of pathos and deep concern because we have been so close to such human need. In writing this book, we give a part of ourselves away. In so doing, it brings us much satisfaction, because we do not only talk about the death of love—but also its rebirth; not only about endings—but also new beginnings; not only about deep hurt—but also true healing.

SUCCESSFUL STEPPARENTING

I

Why Stepfamilies Are Different

Few people realize the complexity of the emotions affecting interaction in the stepfamily. In these two chapters you will be shown the basic myths encountered by many who already live, or contemplate living, in a stepfamily. Also, you will see just how important defense mechanisms are in stepchildren. Just what makes stepchildren tick? Acquiring a basic knowledge and understanding of these two areas is absolutely essential for better relationships within a stepfamily.

1

Confronting the Myths in Stepparenting

So, you're a stepparent or thinking about being one. It is not easy—after you get involved you'll often wonder, *Wow, what's happened . . . this is nothing like I expected.* Step relationships engender tremendous feelings. The following true account will give you some idea of those feelings.

Some time ago, an eleven-year-old lad was in our counseling office. He sat at the opposite end of the sofa from his stepdad. The boy had been brought to us because he was incorrigible both at home and at school. With pronounced body language and a totally defiant inflection in his voice, he angrily shouted at the man seated at the other end, "I don't have to mind you—you're only my stepdad!" Such hateful attitudes are very common.

We saw another stepfather in counseling who related the following experience, which is so typical. He said that he felt great rejection because his stepson of more than eleven years suddenly announced that he no longer wanted to live with him and his mother. Within two days after making the announcement this sixteen-year-old boy was gone. With great hurt and his voice choking with emotion, the stepdad said, "Just think, I poured myself into the life of that boy for years. I loved him and cared a great deal. After all I became like his father. You'd think he'd respect me more. The thing that hurt, too, was that his mother approved of his decision." Although this man felt deep hurt, the mother understood the boy's need to be with his real father, and she gave the approval.

We do not wish to convey the message that every stepfamily has severe problems. Many people express great love and deep appreciation for a stepparent who stepped in when one parent died or there was a divorce. Such testimonials are very heartwarming.

Our experience leads us to believe, however, that very few "ideal" situations just happen—without sweat, toil, and tears. You see, there is probably no more difficult a relationship among human beings than that established by a stepfamily. We are all aware of the mother-in-law jokes. We've also heard about Cinderella and her stepmother. Unfortunately, people really do believe "wicked stepmother tales." This stereotype has been impressed indelibly upon us through the years.

Also, children are pictured as helpless victims. After a recent major professional boxing bout, one sportswriter for a leading American newspaper made the comment that so-and-so "was beaten like a stepchild." Thus the image is perpetuated at all levels of society.

We use the term *stepfamily* where there is a family in which at least one of the adults is a stepparent. The term *step* is the word most frequently used to indicate that the children are the biological offspring of only one or neither of the parents who care for the child. Stepfamilies also differ from the intact family in that the children are often shared with the natural parent who is absent. This can create intense problems because the absent parent will nearly always have a strong influence upon the child, whether by personal contact, telephone, and letters, or merely by being in the memory of the child.

Stepchildren by the Millions

It is not known precisely how many stepchildren there are in the United States. The U.S. Census Bureau still does not include this category in its questionnaires. When asked about this, one census taker commented that "the subject is still too sensitive."

We do know that remarriage rates have risen by 40 percent during the sixties and seventies, while the annual number of divorces during the same years has risen by a whopping 80 percent! Well over half of all divorces involve couples who have children. The Census Bureau states that the average marriage in America today lasts about seven years. That means that a lot of children are going to be hurt at a very tender age. And the problem is mounting—especially in this country, as seen by a recent United Nations report. It indicates that the United States leads all nations on earth in the divorce rate. To be specific, the rate is 5.17 divorces for each 1,000 people.

Because of the growing trends of divorce and remarriage, it is expected that in the eighties over a million new children each year are going to experience the breakup of their parents' marriage. There are estimated, now, to be between 11 and 13 million stepchildren. Since there are about 66 million children under eighteen in this country, it means that about one in every six is a stepchild! Further, that means that if current trends continue at the present pace, by the end of this century more mothers and fathers will be parenting stepchildren than their own!

Not long ago we were testifying in behalf of a client in a custody case in a Los Angeles courtroom. During a recess in the proceedings the judge told us that if things continue the way they're going, by 1990 one-half of the children in vast Los Angeles County will not be living with both of their natural parents.

Some professional counselors and sociologists have projected that during this current decade, at the present accelerated rate, one in every three children will undergo the trauma of the divorce and remarriage of at least one of their natural parents. That means that this social phenomenon is one that has to be acknowledged by all of us. The instability of the American family can no longer be swept under the rug. Nor can Christian families continue to say, "It can't happen to us." It can and is happening with great regularity just as in non-Christian families. So far as we know, there have been no major studies on the comparison of statistics on Christian versus non-Christian divorce and remarriage.

Our contacts in the counseling field report that churchgoing people don't always have the ability to handle the serious problems encountered in breakups or blending two families together in what is commonly called the stepfamily. The reason is that we are not dealing exclusively with spiritual problems when people are traumatized over the loss of the home life they're used to. As Christian counselors, we've discovered that there are psychological truths that Christians need to learn to help them better apply the Bible to their own lives. Human emotions come into play, and they—as well as spiritual principles—must be looked at and understood for what they really are. Attention to behavioral and temperamental problems will have little effect unless the underlying raw feelings are dealt with.

Let us now focus on some of the major myths that are encountered in relation to many stepfamily situations.

Myth #1—You Have to Be Perfect

In looking at ourselves and observing others we have clearly seen that nearly all stepparents have a great need for reassurance. Well-meaning stepparents truly do want to achieve, because they've accepted a major challenge. In fact, some are absolutely consumed with proving themselves. Experientially we'd almost have to say that unrealistic expectations may be the biggest trap for stepparents. What this does is make them very vulnerable to discouragement when things don't work out to their liking.

The first step in preventing attitudes of perfectionism is to realize your limitations. Accept your humanness and always remember that you are dealing with a family that is lacking biological ties. Many people whom we have counseled think that everything will work out because they are familiar with a traditional family system; they are adults; they are loving and eager to give it a try; and they are Christians. But people fool themselves by holding onto high expectations and fantasies such as: "It will be just like having my own kid." In many, many cases that fantasy blows up in a person's face and, inevitably, hurt follows.

You will be way ahead of the game if you accept the idea that initially you are an outsider. Once this reality is recognized and accepted, the stepparent is better equipped to face the possible hurts down the road. Our experience and work with stepparents reveal that it may take years before a strong bond or kinship is created with the stepchildren—if ever.

After years of working with stepfamilies, a husband-and-wife team, June and William Noble, indicate that fanciful expectations do exist and may lead to much trouble ahead. They say that many adults, as they move into their stepparenting role, find it difficult to grasp that living with other people's children means different rules, different expectations, and different solutions.[1]

When we began our own stepfamily, we suffered from very lofty expectations. Even though we had much counseling experience, popular reading material led us to believe that if we just filled our home with lots of love, we could win over all the children in a year or so. Alas, we found that the problems and tensions went much deeper than anticipated.

Adding to our problem was the fact that high expectations were not only held by the world in general but by such groups as the church, relatives, welfare agencies, and counselors: The stepparent is to act just like the real parent.

In her fine book *The Half-Parent,* Brenda Maddox says that stepparenting is little like natural parenting, even though that is what is expected. The clarity, she says, that one finds in natural families is often absent in stepfamilies.[2]

Unrealistic expectations do abound, and they are too numerous to deal with in a book of this kind. But here are just four that will be discussed further along in this book:

1. A stepparent can replace a natural parent.
2. A stepparent must try to meet all the needs for the child that are not being supplied by the absent parent.
3. A stepparent must love the child.
4. The stepchild will respond positively if given love.

These four expectations mislead people when they try to handle problems of stepparenting. Society itself does not provide the answers, because of its own cultural expectations of the family. Solutions can only come from those who are really in the know. We sought assistance from a respected counselor who told us that it was very difficult to set up a stepfamily because there are almost no norms or standards to go by. Trying to be perfect by fulfilling what you think people expect of you can lead to failure and untold guilt.

Myth #2—Children Can Adapt Easily in Stepfamilies

The emotions of stepchildren, we've found, are often more sensitive than those experienced by children in an original family. When a stepchild is jolted by some harsh circumstance—whether by the death of a parent or by the divorce of his parents—he is going to feel it very strongly.

A second myth perpetuates the view that because children are young or are not yet adults, they can easily adapt to any situation, including living in a stepfamily. We have found this is not true. Stepchildren go through incredible trauma—first through the trauma of divorce and then the trauma of the remarriage of their parents. And, the remarriage is almost as big a shock as the divorce. A divorce may shatter the relationship between a child's parents, but he is part of both of them forever. Older people can have new spouses and ex-spouses, but there is no such thing as an ex-mother or an ex-father to a child. He has a parent, alive or dead, in his mind, and that bond can never be severed no matter how his life might be altered in terms of family arrangement.

Also, adapting to change is extremely difficult for many stepchildren because they may be afraid of losing some of their power or responsibilities. For example, a girl who has been used to doing a lot of the cooking or keeping house for her father is probably going to resent another woman's coming in and taking over. A young man who has been used to helping his mother with family responsibilities will possibly resent another man around the house.

Such an intrusion makes adaptation to change so very difficult because it upsets the balance of things. If the family has learned to operate without one of the parents around, it is hard to let someone else come in and take over. Coping with the feelings caused by the intrusion of the new stepparent is a key challenge in those first days, months, and even years of the remarriage.

Conflicting and very intense emotions within a stepchild often make it difficult to deal with change. Because of their frustrations they can become constantly resentful, consistently sly and deceitful. They become extremely defensive, suspecting everyone, and they will often reject offers from those who may make the friendliest gestures to reach out to them.

There is no question that it is much tougher for stepchildren to adapt to traumatic changes, because their fear of abandonment results in less opportunity to deal with their raw, intense emotions.

We need to remember also that children are still children, even though their outward adaptation to complex issues may make them seem like adults in the way they behave and speak. But they still feel and think like children. Although they may appear to have intellectual understanding and even the physical build of adults, their social and emotional maturity usually lags far behind. There is a danger of parents accepting a display of maturity for true maturity. It may be more difficult for older stepchildren, especially, to relinquish their "adult-like" roles, and because of this they may have a greater problem accepting the stepfamily arrangement—viewing the stepparent as an intruder.

Remember, also, that all children will manipulate others for attention or play one parent against another. They will fight with their brothers and sisters in struggling to find their own identity. They will withdraw emotionally when hurt and lash back in anger when they feel rejected. Children in stepfamilies will do the same thing but frequently with more intensity. As we shall see, their defense structures may be so rigid and thick that they have extreme trouble dealing with their emotions. Insecurity is often very great because of what counselors call the double whammy: First there is the tremendous shock of loss in the original family; then comes the remarriage.

Don't forget, too, that unless we are talking about young infants, the problem of adaptability is great for those entering into the stepfamily, because their personalities are already pretty well molded. Basically, they have developed their own sense of needs, wants, habits, and coping mechanisms that may resist change.

John and Emily Visher, two pioneers in stepfamily therapy, explain very well why it is more difficult for stepchildren than for others to adjust to change. Because of their grief and fear of the possibility of another loss, they find it hard to get close in new relationships. This can make them very anxious and guilty whenever they discern tension in the new family.[3]

Once you discard the myth that stepchildren have to be like other children when it comes to acceptance of change, it can alter your whole outlook. When your tolerance level goes up, you can reach out in more caring and helpful ways to your stepchild.

Myth #3—Stepchildren Quickly Get Over Loss

When a child loses a parent, the feelings of loss can be very devastating. It may be felt for years without much letup. There is an erroneous tendency to believe that because a child has gone through great trauma or suffering, he will be better prepared to handle it in an adult fashion.

We counseled a teenage girl whose hurt and pain over her father's leaving had practically destroyed her. She lost all motivation to go on. She stopped singing and playing the piano—activities that had made her father very proud of her. During counseling she sat down and wrote a poem describing her intense feelings of abandonment and loss. Here is her song, used by permission:

Daddy

I once was a part of him
    but now I don't know.
I was able to look at him
    with a special glow.
And then things changed he told me . . .
I cried that night he left
    and then I looked up in the sky
    I had to ask myself, "Why, oh why?"
Oh, Daddy, please don't go away.
    I'm still the same little girl that you knew.
    Oh, Daddy, please don't go away!
And now he's gone,
    but I'll live on somehow.
I'll always remember
    the way I feel right now.
Oh, Daddy, please don't go away.
    Oh, Daddy.
    Oh, Daddy
Oh, Daddy's GONE!

Loss of a parent can be bad enough. But the feelings of loss over the breakup of the original family unit are often increased when a stepparent enters the scene. It is a reminder that things have indeed changed and that they may never revert back to earlier days when there was the security of togetherness.

If you want to know just how children feel about their parent's remarrying, just ask them. One girl told us, "I never want my mother to remarry, and I'll do everything I can to get in the way if she even considers it." This girl's attitude may sound selfish, but it demonstrates how grave is her feeling of loss.

Fortunately, not all children feel this way. For some, Mom's or Dad's remarriage may be the greatest thing that could happen to them. But for most, when parents remarry, the children are bound to feel some jealousy and be envious if the noncustodial parent has bettered his lot in life materially and emotionally. Some children want to share in the new life. Others just do not want any part of it.

Take Jerry, for example. As we counseled him, this eight-year-old boy said that he would never go to the house where his mother and her new husband lived. He absolutely could not accept the fact that his mother had a relationship with a man other than his own father. The only way he would see his mother was alone, away from her home, at a restaurant, park, sporting event, or the like.

Let's not forget that loss is a mourning process for all human beings regardless of age. Few children quickly get over the pain of losing a parent. Those of us in the stepfamily world would do well to allow time for the grief process to heal. Sometimes the loss never heals completely, but we must always respect the child who experiences it.

Myth #4—A Stepfamily Can Operate Like a Normal Family

The most pervasive myth in a remarriage is that the stepfamily can—and should—function like a biological or natural family.

Many people, including psychiatrists and psychologists, who should know better, erroneously make the assumption that parenting and stepparenting are one and the same thing. They are not! When you realize this, you may be well on the right road to deal adequately with the issues ahead. But if you are blinded by this myth, you set yourself up for bitter disappointment, discouragement, disaster—or possibly a divorce.

Stepfamilies really are different! A key or basic difference is that a stepparent has assumed the responsibility for helping to raise another individual's children. Most of us have been conditioned to want our own children—not someone else's.

Another key reason why stepfamilies are different and susceptible to failure is the very nature of groups. Sociology recognizes two basic kinds of groups. First, there is the *primary* group. This is comprised of family and close intimate friends. Second, there is the *secondary* group. These people are those with whom contact is more formal and less personal. Relations are far less intimate in this group.

At the outset, one of the major problems in blending a stepfamily is that you are trying to establish relationships in a primary environment (home) with people who are in the secondary group. The home, which represents an intimate, private area of life where one finds sanctuary and is revitalized, is stressfully invaded when a more formal, distant person from a secondary level is brought into the primary environment. The resulting tension leads to great stress because there's a lack of intimacy, privacy, and feeling of support from a secondary person.

Furthermore, sociologists tell us that the highest form of stress is incurred when an individual feels that he has no control over his life. This is most clearly shown when elderly people enter rest homes and are stripped of almost all responsibility. The idea can be carried through in a stepfamily, where a stepparent may feel so unable to take control that it causes ongoing stress. This feeling of not being in control can be the greatest form of stress for human beings and has caused the demise of many stepfamilies.

Intact families in this fast and demanding society of ours have stress, as we all know. But the structure and emotional stresses are different in stepfamilies. This truth is readily noted by the Vishers, who were among the first to write in depth on stepparenting. They say that disruptions from outside the home impinge on the stepfamily much more than on the natural family. This causes greater stress and unique problems. Those living in a natural family have little comprehension of the strong emotional forces and the difficult tasks that face stepfamily members.[4]

The stresses are bound to come and they are among the major problems facing stepfamilies. It is extremely difficult for individuals to prepare for the stepparenting experience. We are all shown how to be fathers and mothers by our parents, but who ever told us how to be stepparents? Probably in ten or fifteen years this will change as more people become stepparents. More and more books will be written on the subject. College classes will bring us more training, and professional counselors will be forced to face the issue right in their own offices. But for now most people are left to sink or swim on their own.

Try to remember that the blended family is incredibly more complex because of the stressed emotional relationships. We heard one person aptly describe it: "There are too many people in a second marriage. If life in a biological family is like playing a game of chess, life in a stepfamily is like playing five games of chess simultaneously."

Myth #5—Stepmothers Are Wicked Creatures

There is perhaps some small kernel of truth to the fictional idea about "wicked stepmothers." Sometimes a stepmother can be hostile toward her husband's children. Sometimes the children fear her as a competitor and become jealous of her relationship with their father. The stepmother does intrude and she does threaten children's fantasies of their natural parents reuniting. She is all these things and more just because she is there. It may have nothing to do with her character, personality, or values. In most cases stepmothers "can't win for losing." This often is true for stepfathers as well, but usually in a much milder form.

Nearly all literature written on the subject of stepmothers agrees that she becomes the pivotal issue or battleground in the stepfamily. This is primarily true because the home seems always to revolve around the mother figure no matter who she may be. A foster mother would fit the same category. If things go wrong, the finger is usually pointed to the female figure as the culprit.

Maybe the stepmother lends support to the myth because in a sense she "digs her own grave." She probably puts the pressure upon herself by wanting to perform well. By putting her own needs (to be the rescuer) above those of the children, she may blind herself to the real needs of the stepchildren. She makes her mistake by focusing on the things she has to accomplish instead of on the feelings of the children.

A stepmother can be a better cook, housekeeper, and friend than the real mother. She may even believe she has much more to offer the children than the natural mother. But the key issue is not her ability but what the children want! The most common complaint by stepmothers that we hear in counseling is that they feel used and used and used. We hear things like this very often: "I just love John, that's all. I thought I could be a supermom and take care of him and his poor kids. I did it for him because I love him. But it was a grave mistake."

Another thing making the stepmother's role so difficult is the legacy bequeathed to her in the form of past mistakes. One such stepmother felt she was "standing on the ruins of someone else's life, and paying, paying, and paying for her mistakes."

Wicked is hardly the term for most stepmothers. We've found nearly all of them to be very caring persons who really do "have heart." Most have great courage—if they didn't, they would not have accepted the challenge in the first place. Most are honest and sensitive, and nearly all want the best for the children. To consider them "evil" brings a blight to a large segment of our community.

Many Pressures Leave Stepfamilies Vulnerable

The problems experienced by all members of a stepfamily provide one of the greatest challenges in family life today. The emotional pressures in the stepfamily cause an undercurrent of strong feelings that is unique. It is folly to ignore these pressures for the sake of peace and harmony. We've mentioned five major myths or beliefs that need to be dealt with for better stepfamily living. There are still other false ideas that may make such a family more vulnerable. Take for example a father who remarries and keeps his children with him. The stepchildren may (1) believe that his new wife broke up their parents' marriage whether she did or not; (2) think that the new woman is keeping the father from going back to their mother; (3) hold to the idea that the stepmother is either ignorant or just plain dumb because she doesn't do things the way their mom used to.

In addition to myths and beliefs that can interrupt harmony, there are other pressures that make the stepfamily more vulnerable to stress:

1. Because there is a mix of at least two previous families, there are more ideas on how a family should operate.
2. There are more people involved, including another set of grandparents.
3. The absent parent nearly always bears a strong influence upon the family.
4. Because the stepfamily is instant, it has no time to grow and be nourished at the beginning like natural families.

These pressures can create tremendous disharmony. Virginia Satir, in her marvelous book *Peoplemaking*, describes the atmosphere in a troubled family. It is easily recognizable, she says. You can just feel the tension—it is usually cold. The atmosphere may be extremely polite, especially when nonfamily members are around. But you can sense that everyone is bored, or the air is sometimes full of secrecy. There is little evidence of friendship or joy in one another. Bodies are still and tight, or slouchy. Faces look sullen, sad, or blank. People just try to tolerate each other.[5]

This same description applies to stepfamilies and may be even more pronounced.

The late, famous anthropologist Margaret Mead offers a very good general reason why stepfamily relations often are not satisfactory. Her conclusion, following the study of many cultures, is that in the normal, biological family children naturally develop an overdependence on their parents. This, she says, places a great demand on these adults to provide nearly all the security a child may need. The problem just escalates in the stepfamily because we have not made an adequate social or psychological provision for their security and identity outside of the original family should the parents break up.[6]

As stepfamilies face the stresses and problems that are unique to them, children nearly always are the key to success or failure. In our counseling many stepparents tell us that the only time they fight is over the children. Children can do great damage to the adjustment of the newly remarried couple. The children can be experts on knowing how to play one parent against the other. They can accuse parents of favoritism or of being too strict. They can be insulting and competitive.

But in coming to an understanding of why children behave the way they do, it is important to realize that they are very likely to be angry and misbehave until things settle down and they become more aware of the intentions of both parents. They need to test and test in order to see how far they can go as well as to discover for themselves the level of acceptance and love they may expect from the new parent who enters the home. While they test, they will quite naturally create many problems.

There are several key reasons why over 50 percent of second marriages don't make it. The high fatality is due to myths and problems that perhaps may be boiled down to three:

1. Tremendous anger and resentment among all family members
2. Grave hurts experienced by stepparents and the children
3. Granitelike loyalties tenaciously held on to by children for both natural parents

Committing yourself to raising another person's child is a great service and ministry. God saw how important this was. He instructed Moses in the ancient community of Israel to initiate a social pattern for the care of children who had lost a father by death or divorce ("kinsman redeemer").

Despite all the myths and pressures that harass the stepfamily, God has not left us without hope. The Apostle Paul in the New Testament said that: "No temptation [trial] has overtaken you but such as is common to man; and God is faithful, who will not allow you to be tempted beyond what you are able, but with the temptation will provide the way of escape [cope] also, that you may be able to endure it" (1 Corinthians 10:13).

As you are in your stepfamily situation you may be tempted to give up, but if you have an awareness of some of the myths, you can combat them and go on. This awareness is absolutely essential. Remember

. . . you do not have to be perfect

. . . don't expect your stepchildren to adapt easily

. . . your stepchildren may not easily get over feelings of loss

. . . you do not have to function like a biological family

. . . stepmothers are not "wicked" creatures because of their role

Try to back off from blaming yourself for any supposed failure. Rather, try to see that there are differences inherent in the stepfamily, as over against the biological family.

2

What Makes the Stepchild Tick?

Just what is it that makes children tick? All parents would like a better understanding of this, but stepparents may have a greater interest in that question than do others. Statistics bear out the fact that second and third marriages have a higher rate of divorce than the first. There are two main reasons for this: (1) financial problems and (2) the stepchildren.

The children seem to be at the center of the arena for the staging of the intense emotional scenes characteristic of the stepfamily. It makes sense then to try to see what's going on with them and some of the possible reasons for their behavior.

It is our firm belief that parents, as well as professional counselors, cannot clearly understand the stepfamily problem without some knowledge of the defense mechanisms that are used by children. They help us to predict what might happen. Getting insight into these defenses is like "going upstream" to get at the source of a problem. Then you won't just be treating symptoms; you'll be treating causes.

Solutions for bad human behavior are often found in simply identifying the nature or basis of the underlying problem. Sometimes, then, a person can learn to deal with it on his own. The following illustration helps us to see this truth in action. In the Pacific Northwest one of the major industries is lumbering. When trees are felled, they are often sent down flumes to large streams and rivers, which then carry them away to lumber mills downstream. Frequently there are logjams. The men who set out to correct the situation do not spend all their time clearing the jam; they go upstream to see what is creating the problem in the first place.

The sincere and serious parents in the stepfamily will want to look at the source of the troubled areas. Since they have a built-in tendency to internalize everything as personal rejection when things don't go right, looking at the defenses will help them to refrain from overreacting. They will be able to relax in knowing that often simple mischief in a child may only be a reaction to a different circumstance for which he is not responsible. We hasten to add, however, that we do not excuse bad behavior in stepchildren. The key is to know what is causing inappropriate and self-defeating behavior so you can act rationally and properly.

Defense mechanisms are as old as Adam and Eve. We all use them every day of our lives. If we didn't use them, we would have no personal identity. In their very first recorded encounter with God, Adam *denied* blame for his action and put it elsewhere. After he had taken the forbidden fruit from his wife, Eve, God confronted him about his disobedience. Unable to face criticism he used the *denial defense.*

"Who me?" said Adam. "It was Eve who gave it to me!"

Just What Is a Defense Mechanism?

Adults and children alike, when faced with emotional pain or conflict, must find some way to defend themselves against its impact. Defenses are a good thing—we all need them in order to deal with the pressures of life and to maintain a healthy ego. But they can be used in wrong ways too: for instance, when a young child lies because he can't stand the pressure of facing the truth about himself.

A *defense mechanism* is simply a method a person uses to deal with frustration and to organize the stress in his life so he can handle them better.[1]

We can, therefore, see that defenses fulfill a vital purpose—to help a person's ego deal more effectively with reality. When anxiety is felt or anticipated, we either cope and deal with it effectively, or we end up resorting to irrational measures. When defenses are employed in moderation, they are very helpful in dealing with the frustrations and hurts of life. They contribute to our well-being by letting us express ourselves in less costly ways emotionally.

When they are overused or used in unhealthy ways to avoid conflict, then they can be "sick" defenses. A person with a weak ego will rely upon "neurotic" defenses that are either the abuse or failure of a normal one. A defense is abnormal or irrational when it eliminates the responsibility for one's actions. Manipulating others to get affection and drinking excessively to drown sorrow or stress illustrate the wrong use of a defense. Or, take a stepchild who projects all his problems onto others. He may not mature emotionally because he won't ever take the responsibility for his behavior. He may also have a very difficult time growing, changing, and taking his place in the family structure.

Such unhealthy means of coping have the same general effect: They make individuals less aware of the pain—and they lead people to deceive themselves. The reason? Those coping methods become excuses and cover-ups for not acting in responsible ways.

In the final analysis, all defenses may be categorized as means of attacking, withdrawing, compromising, or accommodating to trauma, conflict, or hurt. They protect the self from stress in one or more of the following ways:

1. Denying or restricting experience
2. Changing or distorting reality
3. Reducing emotional involvement
4. Countering threats of hurt or danger

Think of it this way. Defenses are either successful or unsuccessful depending on whether they assist a person to deal with conflict in appropriate ways or not. Remember, too, that defensive reactions may be clung to with unreasonable tenacity. Sometimes it takes therapy to help a person recognize them and do something about them. Defenses are critical, particularly for children in stepfamilies, and the better you understand and can recognize them the better you can cope with the whole situation.

Where Do Defenses Come From?

Psychologists don't know everything about defense mechanisms, but they are fairly well agreed upon one thing, and that is—they develop early in life. Social and behavioral scientists believe that the first emotional adjustments a child makes to his mother and father will form the basis for just about every relationship of life. That is why losing a parent when divorce or death occurs is such a devastating blow to a child.

If a child learns early in life that when something is frightening relief can be obtained by avoiding it, he will no doubt repeat the behavior time and time again. All defenses are learned responses usually picked up from parents, brothers, and sisters. For example, take a boy who may be made fun of at school. He might complain to his father and get the response: "Don't pay any attention to those jerks. You don't need people. Just walk away." That boy learns very early that the best way to deal with situations or people is to isolate or hang labels on his peers. The father in this case passed on to his son the defense of *isolation*—the same way he himself reacted to upsetting experiences.

In adult life the same defenses are called upon that were learned in early childhood. If a child always ran away from fights by going home, he will use *flight* as a defense against anxiety. If that same person, in his teens, would never face confrontation or criticism by a teacher, or as an adult, refuses to "slug it out with the boss," he is locked into the same defense he used as a little boy. Running away from problems has always been his way of dealing with conflict. Until he can break this early learned defense, he will forever remain an immature little boy emotionally when it comes to dealing with confrontation.

It is interesting to realize that neurotics are really people who behave and respond to conflict just as they did as children. The more normal person is able to sort out new experiences in relationships without reenacting or reliving the past.[2]

Children are opportunists. For example, they quickly learn how to manipulate others. Child psychologists agree that the basic orientation of all children is self-serving. That is why they learn so quickly to reduce pain. If you perceive how and why a stepchild is behaving in a certain way, you've taken the first step toward dealing positively with it. Stepchildren can become very adept at manipulation, especially if parents allow it. It may appear on the surface that they enjoy doing this, but it does not provide them with much security or safety over the long haul.

As a stepparent, be encouraged that no one handles the responsibility of dealing with the defenses of their children in a perfect manner. Simply try to understand what is going on—this will make your job easier. Look to your own common sense, too, while providing loving care and discipline.

In stepchildren there are six basic emotions that you will have to recognize. Their defenses spin-off from these:

1. Anger
2. Love
3. Fear
4. Rejection
5. Grief (mourning over a loss)
6. Guilt

Your stepchildren may seek almost any means to relieve the emotional pain they feel. And, much like taking heroin, they may become "hooked" because the defense makes then feel better—at least temporarily. But as with taking drugs, it may ultimately make matters worse.

Psychology Can Be a Good Tool

We realize that talking about defense mechanisms and other psychological terms may be a bit unfamiliar and boring to you. Some people might even say, "Psychology turns me off." Others might add, "Don't give me psychology; just give me the Bible." We just want to say that our personal viewpoint is strongly biblical. But from our study of human behavior we can see that psychology is like any other science; it is neither good nor bad. It is simply truth that anybody can use in order to live a more effective life.

Whether we want to admit it or not, our mind—particularly our unconscious mind—has tremendous power over us. By the term *unconscious,* we refer to that part of the mind that psychologists call the *memory bank.*

There are many times in the stepfamily relationship that you'd bet your life that your child is *willfully* acting in a certain way. That is not always true. Remember that children imitate the adults around them, and that process does not really end until they become adolescents or teenagers. Then they may try to throw away some of their parents' attitudes and values. But children, because they don't have the vocabulary or the conceptualized ability to put labels onto their emotions and beliefs, push many things into the unconscious.

So then, it all boils down to this: Your stepchild may not even realize he is using defense mechanisms, and perhaps you haven't realized it either. That's what this book is all about. We are not trying to make you into an amateur psychologist, but we *are* trying to help you understand your stepchild and become a better stepparent.

How a Child Uses Defenses to Cope With Loss

The feeling of loss is one of the greatest traumas experienced by human beings. This includes children. To a child his family is everything. Adults may be able to find other avenues of escape or security, but all a young child has is his family. When his family is fractured, the child's sense of security and selfhood also cracks. Both parents are involved in sustaining the child over difficult times. When one of them leaves, "the child is yanked out of proportion. . . . He's supported on one side, and the other side is left hanging."[3]

The loss of security and the "left hanging" feeling is well illustrated by a letter we received from a ten-year-old girl while we were writing this book. Here in her own words are excerpts from that letter:

> Remember me . . . my mom and I came and talked to you about my real dad. I sent him a Father's Day card but received no reply. I wrote one or two more letters after that but nothing ever came. I wish he would write me since I haven't moved and he knows my address. I wish he would write because I'm not mad at him and I love him. Do you think he still loves me?
>
> Still Waiting

Children will try to cope with loss in various ways. Some will not always show their feelings, and adults will have the tendency to discount the seriousness of the problem. Children will quite naturally carry any scars and the bewildered memories of the loss right into the stepfamily picture.

Would you believe that when a child is brought into a stepfamily, the separation anxiety over the loss of a parent may become even stronger? Old fears come alive, and new ones come to the surface that can aggravate the situation. The stepchild is literally surrounded by a world of uncertainties:

1. Who am I now?
2. Where do I belong?
3. Will I lose my mother or father to this person he or she is marrying?
4. Can I like this new stepparent and still love my other parent?

Such fears are usually reinforced rather than calmed in the new marriage.[4] This happens because when a remarriage occurs and other children are brought into the picture, the familiar structure is swept away. A child who once was the oldest may now be next to the oldest or the youngest. An only child may suddenly have two or three brothers or sisters. This can upset the balance.

If the stepchild is paralyzed by a set of fears about the future, you may expect that he could very well express his feelings in very inappropriate ways. There may be sudden mood changes. There may be crying or tantrums or a sudden drop in school grades. There may be antisocial behavior or just quiet withdrawal. All of these are quite evident in all children under stress. They are much more to be expected in stepchildren.

Because of the separation of his original parents, the stepchild is so disturbed that he will test and test again to prove to his satisfaction that things will be all right. Such a child already believes that his parents have failed to live up to the ideal of what a family is all about, so he has to find reassurances in the new family.

The implications of the feelings of loss are often far-reaching. Some children have confessed to us that they also feel disappointed in themselves, and they worry about whether they should get married or whether anyone will be able to love and marry them when they grow up. Others believe that somehow they caused the breakup of their parents. One eight-year-old told us: "If anything bad happened to me, then I must have deserved it."

We have come to believe, through our counseling with stepfamilies, that younger children have a better chance of making good adjustment than do older ones because they trust adults more. Also, older children's defenses are more set because they have adjusted to their natural parents.

One stepmother told us: "One of the major considerations in marriage to a man with children is to look at their ages. Older children, say beyond twelve, will be more sarcastic, know-it-all. At least that was the way it was in our family. The smaller children are much more moldable. It was so much easier to deal with Jack's six-year-old than his fifteen-year-old daughter."

Also, we have come to realize that if a stepparent is immature emotionally, he may be highly demanding of time with the spouse. This can also reinforce the fears of loss in the children that they may lose the natural, custodial parent. The stepchild will then see the new parent as an intruder—"You're taking my mother away from me." This can lead to a lot of manipulation and to power plays in the home for attention. This in itself will create an undue amount of tension.

Fear is not the only problem emotion in stepchildren when they try to deal with loss. Anger may be very evident, and this can set in motion several defensive tactics to deal with it. For example, some release anger symbolically through games (such as "war"). They may release it through sporting events. They may project it onto others ("Kids always pick on me"; "It's their fault"). Powerful dreams and nightmares may be very frequent.[5]

Regardless of the emotion expressed over loss, a child's behavior may be manifested in a multiple of ways, including:
1. Hypersensitivity
2. Aggressive hostility
3. Agitated states seen as nervousness
4. Hyperactivity
5. Lonerism

Some of the effects of a child's behavior over loss are:
1. The masking of real feelings that are eventually manifested in destructive ways
2. Actions that are very juvenile
3. Encroachment on parents' personal privacy by seeking to come between the spouses

Dealing With Loss of Self-Esteem

A child's identity lies with both of the natural parents. When one goes, a part of him goes. The biological parents provide for children a sense of *who* and *what* they are. Therefore, when there is a separation, it represents a loss of love. The feelings of rejection can be most serious. When a part of the child "leaves" through separation, the conflicts will nearly always create a shaking of the sense of self.

It's a blow to self-esteem for the child because he has not had time in life to build his own confidence system through successes and achievements. The child basically measures self-worth by the responses of those around him. The loss of a parent is easily interpreted by the child to mean that "something must be wrong with me or so-and-so wouldn't leave me." These insecure feelings are fertile ground for the growth of defense mechanisms.

Trying to enhance self-esteem, the child will try to win acceptance by his natural parents. This can lead to fierce loyalty conflicts. Caught between giving love to the natural parent who is absent and trying to find a place for the stepparent, the child unknowingly may use a defense so he won't have to deal with the negative conflicts and feelings.

The Mind Can't Stand Mystery

One reason defenses are formulated in stepchildren is that when the original family structure is missing, they are frequently left in the dark about what really happened. Their questions may go unanswered for years. The bewilderment and confusion leads them to draw their own conclusions, which can be either right or wrong.

The human mind likes things signed, sealed, and delivered. None of us likes uncertainty. We don't like loose ends. The fear of the unknown can be very disturbing. For all of us, when there is some unsatisfactory or unexplainable situation, the "law of closure" becomes operative. The mind will seek to find closure—it will close the gap with one or more assumptions because the mind can't stand mystery.

Don't ever make the mistake of saying, "My child is not old enough to understand," (unless he is a tiny infant) or, "He won't really be affected by what's going on."

Little do parents realize what's going on inside their youngster's head. The child will always seek to close the information gap somehow, and this can lead to irrational defensive measures. That's why it can be very detrimental to require children to hide their true feelings or hurt, as some parents suggest, behind a facade of good manners. That's just asking for trouble.

One of the basic truths that all people entering into a stepfamily relationship must realize is that nearly every child who is confronted by a prospective stepparent is going to have some kind of anxiety. Certainly, one major problem in remarriage is the tendency of parents not to allow honest and true feelings all around. They are so afraid of discord and tension they may adopt the "head in the sand" policy about negative feelings.

In this book we are going to cover nine basic defense mechanisms used by children. Because some of the defenses have similar features, identifying them with a particular behavior pattern is not always clear-cut.

You will notice that the discussion in each chapter has a threefold emphasis:
1. What defense mechanism is being used?
2. What are some of the characteristic behavior patterns seen in the stepchildren as they use the defense?
3. What can parents do about the problems caused by the defense mechanism?

II

The Stepchild Who Just Tunes Out

Many parents in the stepfamily know what it's like to have stepchildren who seem to be running from reality. It's what is called *flight*. In the next three chapters you will be introduced to such psychological terms as *repression, denial,* and *reaction formation.* Don't let these terms throw you. They all have to do with very basic questions that are asked in many homes. Questions such as:

1. Why does my child act as though there is nothing wrong, when I know there is?
2. Why does my child seem to cover over the truth about what has happened in the past?
3. Why does my child seem to play a role by acting in extreme ways?

3

"I'll Forget It; I'll Just Forget Everything"

The tendency for most stepchildren who have been
hurt is to try to push the trauma out of their minds
by the use of *repression*. The trouble is that this
defense may come back to haunt them in many
ways.

"Dr. Juroe, I'm afraid my stepdaughter is going to drop out of
school. She has developed severe headaches and dizziness. She doesn't
seem to want to be with her friends any more. Her father and I are be-
side ourselves. I hope that you can get to the bottom of this because it
can just ruin Linda—set her back socially. And we don't want to have
her repeat a grade in school.

"We have checked with a neurologist, and he's convinced that she
has an emotional problem—not a physical one. Do you have any
suggestions?"

After talking with this distraught stepmother, I arranged to have her
eleven-year-old stepdaughter come in to see me. During her very first
session Linda began opening up.

"I guess the worst problem I have is my mother, who has totally
forgotten about us kids. She married some dumb guy. She spends all
her money on herself, so she has nothing left over for us. Besides, she
hardly ever contacts us."

"How does that make you feel toward your mother?"

"Not so good. When your own mother rejects you, it's pretty lousy. I try not to think about her at all, but whenever I do, I get the crazies. She's such a creep."

Linda came in for more sessions. Every time she'd talk about what happened that day and what was going on with her friends, she tried her best to keep it light. Several more sessions went by. One day we asked, "Linda, you haven't talked about your mother for quite a while. What's going on?"

"Oh, nothing, I haven't heard from her for a long time—I wish she were dead!" After a slight pause she said, "I feel guilty that I even said it."

"That may be so, but it is best you face that feeling and the reasons for triggering it. You have some strong feelings about that don't you?"

"Yes, and you know that is the first time I have ever said that to anyone. I just wish sometimes she'd drop out and get totally out of my life and mind."

Here was a young girl who unconsciously desired that her mother would be harmed in some way. She even imagined her getting hurt. We encouraged her to talk to her parents more about those intense feelings. Her headaches diminished remarkably in several months as she talked more about her mother. She even began to feel better toward her as she tried to understand her.

What Was Wrong With Linda?

Linda's problem was rather serious, for she was trying to forget everything about her mother. She was in the grips of what psychologists call *repression*. By this it is meant that she was trying to put her hurt and anger toward her mother at a distance because she couldn't face them.

Repression is a process whereby a person pushes away hurtful ideas or emotions from his conscious mind. It is quite simply an avoidance technique, and a person treats the unhappy memories of trauma as though they were totally nonexistent.

Repression is perhaps the "granddaddy" of the defenses and can be illustrated in many ways. People have actually experienced some great catastrophe such as a flood or an earthquake, have somehow stumbled in a stupor into a first aid station, and then forgotten everything that had transpired. One psychiatrist says that repression is more than just forgetting something. It is forgetting that we have forgotten.[1]

Usually we do not consciously choose to repress. We do it automatically in those areas where we may be hurt by some person or event. We might remember the event, but the emotion gets repressed. At this point, a distinction should be made between forgetting and repressing:

... Repression is much more complete and permanent. If we forget something, we can easily be reminded of it. A service station, a radio commercial, or an oil truck can remind us to buy gasoline. Thinking about dinner or our children can remind us to buy a quart of milk. When something is repressed, reminders usually do not work. We resist being reminded of our repressed feelings or memories even if they are obvious to other people.[2]

Repression, over a period of time, will shut off the pathways to other emotions and once that happens, we don't even know what we want. A person who is repressed consistently blocks negative or bad feelings and in time will find it difficult to actually feel love.

We've seen this frequently in stepchildren we've worked with. Once they can identify some of their nagging, negative feelings, they can begin to reach out to a stepparent they may have intensely disliked before. We have to realize that repressed feelings don't just go out of existence. Wishing them away doesn't work.

Linda's story discloses how repression can affect us. Time and time again we see stepchildren who do not handle the new family situation very well. Many suffer from physical illnesses that are diagnosed by medical doctors as simply psychosomatic. The likelihood is very strong that repressed negative ideas, thoughts, or feelings will in time show up in some physical ailment. The psychologist calls this *conversion anxiety*. In most cases such disorders are very real and they do need medical attention.

Stepfamilies quite naturally are a prime arena for repressed feelings, because when a stepparent arrives on the scene, a myriad of changes can be expected. The children may become very stubborn and uncooperative. Such negative behavior may be due to the child's repressing of three major problem emotions: anger, grief, and guilt. Most stepchildren experience these emotions, and there is a strong likelihood that they may try to repress them to overcome their hurts. Many of the problems we've seen in stepfamilies are due to these three repressed emotions. Let us look at these one at a time.

"I Don't Know Why I'm So Cold Toward Her"

We've seen many cases where a child will ignore or repress the anger he really feels. Such anger is usually triggered by either frustration or hurt of some kind. Many children will develop deep resentment about the breakup of their parents and will unconsciously try to sabotage the remarriage. That's one way repressed anger will show itself. And, in an effort to make the new stepparent feel he doesn't belong, the child will stay uninvolved with the family, particularly with the stepparent. How many times have we heard a stepmother say, "I feel like I'm just a housekeeper around here"?

Repression in stepchildren not only shows up in aloofness but in many other ways, such as *acting out* behavior. They may steal and lie. Acting out behavior will be discussed more fully when we look at the defense of displacement.

Anger that is ignored usually spews out in small doses and in ways a person may least expect it. Sharon, a beautiful high-school sophomore from a middle-class family, came to counseling because she had few friends left. This puzzled her very much. We found that she had much unresolved anger toward her stepfather and mother, who, she reported, "screwed up my life miserably."

Sharon overreacted to many irritations she found in her friends all because she let resentment build up toward her folks. Through counseling she learned that when she blew up at a friend who was only ten minutes late, it was probably because she had pent-up emotions for some other reason.

One reason some stepchildren try to ignore repressed anger is that they are afraid that it might get out of control. Others may hold back because they're afraid of rejection.

When we counsel youngsters who we suspect may have repressed anger, we attempt to help them realize that repressed anger in the long run will bring about more hurt in relationships. In most cases it is better to express it than to avoid it.

Repressed anger can also be unleashed toward the self in the form of self-hate. A person is usually unaware that this is happening. Frequently, because stepchildren fear to express themselves, the anger has no other place to go. Upset because they cannot get control, the stepchild might get into drugs, overeat, or turn to alcohol or illicit sex. Such destructive behavior is more often than not inner rage turned onto the self.

Then too, the unsettling experience of the death or divorce and remarriage of parents while a child is quite young, say four to seven, may surface again during the rebellious teen years when the natural need for independence and assertiveness arises. These natural, growing needs mixed with the buried emotional pain can be unleashed with great fury upon the parent retaining custody and the stepparent alike. The youth may be very resentful that he had no choice in the decisions pertaining to the breakup of his family. This may aggravate the normal drive for independence—even to the point where the youth gets in trouble with the law.

Remember—repressed anger blocks love. A stepchild may want to reach out to his stepparent but can't. Intellectually he may realize he should and may even appreciate deeply what that person has done or is doing for him and the natural parent in the home but still be unable to feel anything emotionally.

"I Can't Face It . . . I Know I Broke Up My Folks' Marriage"

Guilt—the second emotion that is often repressed in stepchildren is not very easy to detect. When such a child has guilt, it is usually because he believes that he had something to do with the divorce of his parents in the first place or with causing tension and strife in the new home.

Peter, a fiery red-haired youngster, once told us that he hoped his new stepfather would die. Remembering such thoughts brought on great feelings of unworthiness. He had a very difficult time admitting to such thoughts, so he tried totally to forget them. Yet he was down most of the time and couldn't explain why.

We have discovered that most stepchildren have a tendency to repress guilt if they believe they have been somewhat responsible for their parents' breakup. Sometimes the same repressed guilt causes stepchildren to set themselves up for failure. You might see your stepchild alienating himself from church friends, school chums, or neighborhood pals. He might displease the school principal or church youth minister, or he might deprive himself of many pleasures. He may also willfully upset his parents—all to relieve his guilt.

Another way you as a parent may suspect repressed guilt is if your child is depressed a great deal. Guilt is the inability to forgive oneself. If the child believes he cannot control what has happened and holds himself responsible, he may turn inward as a form of punishment.

Discipline helps to relieve guilt, but it is important for parents to be sensitive at first about overdoing punishment. Be sensitive and try to find a good balance in your discipline methods.

If a stepchild comes too much under the tyranny of the "shoulds," it can cause havoc. If stepchildren already have guilt, new demands can make them feel more guilty. One woman in her mid-thirties who grew up in a stepfamily stated that her new blended family was like being in prison. She stated: "I know my father and stepmother thought it was best to crack down. But now I feel guilty about everything. I feel guilty for just existing. I should never have been born." Such unresolved guilt made it very difficult for her own marital adjustment in adulthood.

Needless to say, we don't want stepchildren to repress guilt. Guilt is needed by all. It's a normal emotion, and the Bible tells us the Holy Spirit induces it to bring us closer to God. Some modern therapies attempt to get rid of it, giving people the notion that almost anything goes. But guilt serves a vital function for emotional and spiritual health. Guilt helps to cleanse the mind and soul as well as to enhance change within a person.

"I Don't Want to Face Feelings of Sadness"

Grief is the third major problem emotion that stepchildren will repress. This feeling represents loss, and it may be the most difficult one of all for the stepchild to deal with. In this book we shall be alluding to this emotion many times because of its significance. Mourning, or grief, runs very high and most stepchildren will hide it by presenting a tough outer shell.

Parents in stepfamilies complain frequently that at times their stepchild seems very indifferent to what goes on in the family. The blasé attitude in the children seems to be the predominant trait early in the stepfamily experience. Stepparents often interpret this to mean rejection of themselves. That may not be it at all.

This apparent disinterest in life in general is one way the stepchild deals with loss. In response to the child's attitude, stepparents also may begin to repress their own feelings. Loss or rejection and anger can cause the parent to pull away too. If his overtures of caring and love are scorned, it may cause him to put a lid on his true feelings. Then the natural parent who feels he has to serve as a buffer between his child and the stepparent doesn't want any more trouble either. So feelings all around are stifled.

Many stepchildren, especially the younger ones, will not only show indifference in their battle to combat sadness but may also have sleeping problems. All children go through various phases in their psychological development. It is, for example, to be expected that at certain times they may experience nightmares, which may be a clear indicator that the stepchild is trying to deal with repressed or unresolved grief. You may expect this in children around the ages of four to seven. Frequently, these vivid dreams are seen as abnormal. But it is one of nature's ways to help individuals work through repressed conflicts. When a child has repeated nightmares it is a clue that he is trying to adjust to the losses of separation by repressing his hurts. Like anger and guilt, grief is a valid human emotion. But it's what we do with it that makes the difference in our emotional lives.

When anger, guilt, and grief are not adequately dealt with in stepchildren, they may lead to depression, withdrawal from life, and psychosomatic illnesses. Recognizing and handling those problem emotions in a sympathetic manner takes insight and care, but helping your child to avoid repression will pay handsome dividends later on.

"I've Got a Stomachache"

As we noted earlier, in Linda's case, physical problems or complaints may be a sure sign that the stepchild might be repressing some hurt from the past. They often have headaches, stomachaches, flulike pains, vomiting, and diarrhea. The wise parent will regard those illnesses as real even though they may not result from a virus or other medical factor.

When there are anxiety-induced illnesses, the child is converting unresolved anxiety by escaping into sickness. The child, of course, does not set that up on purpose most of the time—but he might. By getting ill he will receive more attention.

If ever there was a Huckleberry Finn type of boy it was rough-and-tumble Tommy. This nine-year-old was brought into counseling by his parents because he complained of constant stomach pains. His parents took him to several doctors. Finally, one consented to give the boy an "upper GI" exam. The results were negative. After examining him completely, the doctor announced, "Tommy is in perfect health." Suspecting emotional stress as the cause of Tommy's pains, the doctor recommended therapy.

It took only a few sessions to get at the bottom of the whole problem. Tommy was being lectured to by the significant adults in his life. He couldn't get along with his stepfather, so he was being torn apart over the issue of where he should live. He had an intense loyalty conflict. The confusing advice Tommy had received made him very uptight. Once it was decided and he was told, "You are going to live with your mother," he began to relax and to adjust by being able to put his roots down. His stomach trouble cleared right up.

As we've indicated, unresolved anger, guilt, grief, and even fear may contribute to psychosomatic illnesses. If they go unexpressed over long periods of time, the stepchild may experience moods of hopelessness and unworthiness. The result is often in such outward expressions as nervous tics, constant twitching, nervous tapping of hands or feet, nail biting, hair twisting, or other means of getting attention from adults.

Repressed feelings can also show up in such common maladies as ulcers, muscle aches, headaches, allergies, and even the common cold. When stepchildren are allowed to express their true emotions, it is amazing how rapidly they recover, in most instances, from physical problems.

"I Don't Want to Go to School"

A common behavior seen in stepchildren, particularly in adolescents, is the refusal to go to school. This can be a serious problem for parents and creates much tension in the home. Stepchildren often complain of stomach cramps or headaches before leaving for school. These "illnesses" give them some assurance that they will get attention and won't be cast away. In a stepchild the fear of going to school may be a clue that he is repressing some thoughts or feelings regarding the family situation.

We've looked at several basic problems and concerns that arise when repression is present. Now, let's look at some practical things you can actually do about it.

What Parents Can Do

Guideline #1—Be aware of the stepchild's past hurts.

One of the basic things you've got to remember is that the stepchild has been hurt. Divorce or death takes its toll. The child's past family traditions and life have been disrupted. Such children may freeze emotionally at the time tragedy strikes. This will make them less mature and nearly always more sensitive emotionally than those growing up in an intact or stable family.

You must make allowance for the immaturities and insecurity. Give the child the time and space needed for him to follow his own developmental and coping pace.

The following advice is well-taken:

> As a new stepparent you must have the expectation that you may be treated as a temporary guest for quite some time. Even if you feel you have established good rapport with the children before the marriage, do not assume your new role as stepparent will be welcomed overnight.
>
> If you enter an established family, do not expect gratitude for

taking on such heavy responsibilities. You may be a great financial asset, a super repairman/cook/entertainer, but the normally self-centered child will show no gratitude. Well, the child may show a little, but don't count on it.[3]

There may be a lot of repressed feelings that will prevent the child from reaching out at first. It is essential that you remember this. Be aware that your stepchild may never reach out. Your expectations of stepparenting must be based on reality. Because you are in love with one of his parents does not in any way guarantee that he will be open with you.

Guideline #2—Accept the feelings of your stepchild.

Frequently stepchildren have strong feelings of anger, guilt, or sorrow, and they really can't express them. Just be aware of this and encourage your child to talk about those feelings.

It is extremely important, also, for all stepparents to realize that almost every child confronted by a prospective stepparent is going to be an anxious child. In all of our premarital counseling, we have never found one exception to this. About the only way to reach an anxious child is to let him know that his parents understand.

Helen Thomson hits the nail on the head when she says:

> If a youngster is totally happy about his stepparent from the moment they meet, that's fine. But if he can't feel that way, for whatever reason, then it's far, far better to help him express his doubts and his resentments than to require him to hide his troubled feelings. Hidden feelings stay alive and almost invariably find expression in a way that can make parents anxious and youngsters unhappy. Excessive shyness, temper tantrums, health problems, general irritability, these are all problems that can be rooted in insecurity. So in the long run, it's far easier on both parents and children if "bad" feelings are dealt with directly.[4]

Remember that everyone has a right to his feelings. To deny them or discount them in another person is a very cruel thing. The "you shouldn't feel that way" messages given to children only teach them not to face their true selves. Bear in mind that emotions are not good or bad, right or wrong. Only attitudes and behavior are good or bad, right or wrong.

A heartening example of a stepfather who could accept his stepson's feelings is Bob. Here's a stepfather who is really in touch. We asked eight-year-old Ricky about this. "Because my new dad just listens, I can get very upset but he never gets mad back at me. I remember one time when I jumped out of my father's car and came screaming into the house, 'I hate you, I hate you,' to my stepfather, Bob. 'You have no right telling my dad to bring me home early. He's my dad and you're not.' Then my stepdad asked very quietly, 'Why are you so mad Ricky?'

" 'I just wanted to stay at his house longer and watch TV, but you made me come home.' Bob answered me, 'I can understand why you'd be upset. I'm sure it is a lot of fun being with your dad, but the last three times you came home very late and you had great trouble in getting up the next morning to get ready for school.'

" 'You're not my dad, you're not my dad,' I screamed back. Bob just said, 'I realize I'm not your real dad, but I still care for you, your grades, and your health.' "

While telling this story, Ricky smiled shyly, knowing deep down that his stepfather was right, and he is grateful as he looks back to two years ago. Because of his stepfather's total acceptance, Ricky feels very safe and secure. He is indeed a most fortunate youngster.

By allowing the expression of feelings, a stepparent can be a real catalyst in helping a child through the transitional times. The parent should (1) try to understand the reason behind the feeling; (2) accept the emotion as valid; (3) help the child communicate it; and (4) help the child to discharge the feeling in an appropriate manner.

*Guideline #3—**Encourage communication.***

There is no better way to get at repressed feelings than to encourage and permit communication. We'd suggest as a starter weekly family-counsel meetings. It is best to let every person have his say without interruption or interpretation. This is a good place to teach your children how to ventilate their emotions effectively.

If you suspect that your stepchild has a problem of repressing and won't talk even though you know something is wrong, you must develop good communication skills. Effective communication means both talking and listening. Be willing to express your personal thoughts and feelings, but listen! True listening is when a person wants to hear what the other person is saying more than wanting himself to be understood. It's easy to cut a child off by giving your own interpretation or beginning some kind of lecture. That will usually end talking right there. Remember that communication is a two-way process! The less judgmental you are about the child's feelings the more he will talk. Forcing your own values and opinions too early will be counterproductive.

The ideal is to get your stepchild talking. But remember, if you try to force the issue for interaction, your chances for success are greatly diminished. "When you're ready to talk, Billy," is in most cases a better approach than, "Look here, Billy, you're going to sit right down here and I don't care how long it takes to get this out in the open." In most cases this accomplishes nothing.

The following skills, when mastered, will greatly enhance the communication process with your stepchildren:

1. Allow ventilation. Let people unwind, let off steam, or rehash a day's events.
2. Really listen to what someone is saying and grasp the main ideas being expressed. Listen without interpretation. You don't always have to analyze.
3. Learn to recognize all the many assumptions your stepchildren make. Many of them are incorrect. These need to be graciously pointed out to them.[5]

You must allow the children to express their feelings with complete freedom from retaliation, recrimination, or punishment. This enhances the flow. If their behavior is destructive, such as throwing or breaking things, confront them, but still work on allowing the expression of feelings. If you are so insecure that you can't handle their feelings, then *you* may need to go for help. If, for example, you don't handle your own anger over the divorce very well and are too upset to deal with your own losses and heartaches, your stepchildren will sense that. This may have the effect of driving them deeper into themselves.

In the long run, it is probably best not to inflict your intense emotions upon your children. Find adults who will listen to you. Most children do not have the ability to take care of themselves emotionally, let alone having to deal with an adult's emotional problems.

Guideline #4—*Confront bad behavior.*

When a child might be repressed but is misbehaving because there is no other place for those hidden feelings to go, acceptance is vital. However, stepchildren need to be told that their behavior is unacceptable when they depart from the house rules or the standards set before them by the parents.

In our day and age we adults are sometimes so psychologically sophisticated that we refuse to deal properly with bad behavior in our children. Children need discipline. If for fear of rejection or retaliation we handle every situation with stepchildren with kid gloves, we may actually make it worse for the child. If we are so nice that the children don't get the message that their parents are upset, we end up hurting the child. He needs to know the true feelings of the natural parent and the stepparent.

Confronting bad behavior helps the child to get rid of his guilt. That means less repression. Even if a child justifies his behavior most of the time, he knows when he's done wrong. Proper punishment helps to atone for the misdeed and brings psychological relief.

Guideline #5—*Allow your stepchildren freedom in both homes.*

Some children have real problems going back and forth from the custodial parent's home to that of the absent parent. They may never utter a word about it, but children we've seen sometimes admit to feeling guilty when they go "to that other house," especially when that absent parent has been put down a lot. This may prevent the child from enjoying the visitation time.

The stepchild may think of the parent who is left behind. The best way to handle this is to encourage your child when he is away "to forget about us here and make the best of your time when you're with your daddy." This will definitely relieve much pressure, tension, and any sting of guilt. Let the child go without intimidation. Then he won't be so afraid of sharing himself with you. This will greatly minimize repressed feelings.

*Guideline #6—**Consider sound biblical advice.***

God's Word encourages openness at all levels. The apostle Paul, especially in his letters to the early Christians, discusses the necessity of expressing anger, bitterness, malice, and many other negative emotions. Repressed, such feelings could cause harm to the churches. It is no less true in our homes.

Solomon, in an ancient proverb, touched on the bad effect of repression when he said: "He who conceals hatred has lying lips . . ." (Proverbs 10:18).

Questions That Need Answering

1. Could my children be repressing their true feelings?
2. Do I overreact to my stepchild's feelings? How?
3. Have I encouraged my children to discuss their feelings of loss? When?
4. Does my child have physical complaints that might be emotionally induced?
5. Do I make my stepchild feel guilty?
6. Do I encourage open communication in our home?
7. Do I repress my own feelings and thus teach my stepchild to repress his? Am I a bad example?

4

"Someday My Dad Will Come Back"

Because for stepchildren the truth often hurts, they
may *deny* it. Such children are hard to deal with
because they refuse to accept the facts about their
new life in the stepfamily.

"I have seen a ten-year-old girl several times," said a physician to us
some time ago, "and I'm puzzled about what might be wrong with her.
Both she and her mother complain that the girl is constantly tired and
appears to be run down. There's no anemia, and honestly, I find nothing physically wrong with her. There's no reason on the surface for her
lack of energy. I think you should see if you can find out what is going
on."

Something indeed was going on! In the very first session Sheila
began to talk about her real problem. "Doctor Juroe, I think I hate my
dad. He really hurt us when he divorced Mom and moved away. We
never hear from him."

"Well, why is that bothering you so much?" I asked.

"Because it's just not like him. He was so interested in Mom and us
kids. I know he's married to that other woman, but someday he's going
to come back—don't you think?"

"Tell me, Sheila, do you ever have dreams about your daddy?"

"Oh, yes, all the time. Even last night I dreamt that I was sitting on
his lap in our living room, and Mother was smiling as she sat in the
chair next to us. It was so real, the dream I mean, that I couldn't

believe it. I really think that someday it's going to be like that again. It just can't be any other way, can it?"

What Was Sheila Doing?

This young girl was using what is called *denial*. Unable to accept what had happened, she somehow believed that her dad would return home someday and things would be as they once were. Sheila could not accept the fact that her father had remarried and that he was gone—yes, gone for good!

We helped Sheila talk about the realities of her situation. It hurt her even though we tried as gently as possible to tell her that her father probably would never return to live in their house again. Sheila also could see that she was mad at her daddy, even though that was extremely hard for her to admit. For a long time she denied her anger. The denial of anger, too, can make an individual very tired. Once Sheila could begin to accept the truth about her father's new life, her energy level picked up and her school grades went up remarkably as well.

In a way, the defense of denial is an extreme form of repression. Sheila had a hard time admitting to certain feelings, so it was much easier to either deny them or distort the truth about her father's relationship with her. Her story helps us more clearly to define this defensive tactic. Denial basically is the refusal to accept an unpleasant or threatening thought or feeling, even though it may be accompanied by what would ordinarily be convincing evidence.

Sheila had been told by her mother and stepfather at least a hundred times that her daddy was gone forever. This didn't seem to have much impact upon her, because she had a tremendous need to reduce her feelings of anxiety. She was also trying to protect her self-esteem. Wishing and hoping her father would someday come back enabled her to believe that she was worthy of his return.

We might reasonably call the denial defense a great big pain pill. It does deaden trauma and reduce anxiety, usually in one of two ways: (1) by denying the actual existence of some threatening situation or (2) by denying the fact that one feels afraid, hurt, or frustrated.

There isn't one of us who does not use denial to some degree. "That can't be" or "I don't believe it" are often-heard statements. When you analyze such statements, you can see the defense at work in yourself.

When kids are young, they use denial because it's one of the best ways for them to cope. When they grow older, they don't need to use the defense as often because their minds and egos have developed. This makes them more capable of coping with reality. When people get older, they usually are more willing to face facts and not deny them.

Let's face it—denial does work at first. It can be a very useful means of avoiding the psychological pain brought on by deep hurt, as we saw with Sheila. Children as well as adults will try to block out the conscious awareness of hurt. For the moment, it helps because the unconscious mind takes over until a person is ready to deal with the new reality in a healthier way.

But over the long haul denial does not contribute toward coping. This is especially true in a stepchild, who is placed at the mercy of events and other people. Denial therefore can be a destructive force because it hinders a person from identifying, changing, or adjusting to events.

The stepfamily is one of the areas of human existence where we can readily see evidence of denial at work. This presents a great challenge for natural and stepparents. Awareness of the problems that children create by using denial is crucial. Following are some of the typical problem areas you might expect if your child uses this defense.

"I Don't Want You Around Here"

Denial of the new stepparent in a child's family is one of the most prevalent problems that must be faced. In nearly every stepfamily we have ever worked with in our counseling practice, this condition has existed in one form or another when there has been a divorce. Unless a stepparent is extremely aware that this is perfectly natural or is mature enough to deal with this problem, he may have tremendous difficulties in his own adjustment to the blended family.

During one counseling session a stepmother complained to us that her twelve-year-old stepdaughter, Lisa, constantly tried to come between her and her husband. If they were in a serious discussion, she'd enter the room and not leave until sternly told to do so. If the three of them went to Disneyland, Lisa would always try to walk between the two of them.

"I just have the feeling I don't count for much," the mother sadly stated. "Lisa almost denies my right to exist, it seems."

In reality, that's exactly what Lisa was doing. She was not accepting her new stepmother. She didn't want her around. She did want to keep her away from her father. She was trying to drive a wedge between them because she believed her stepmother was an intruder—she did not belong.

The denial of a new parent's existence can come out in other ways as well. Sullenness, silence, fresh remarks, lack of common courtesy, and open belligerence can all mean the same thing: "You shouldn't be here. You have taken the place of someone else who rightly belongs here, and I don't like it one bit."

The stepchild can also deny the stepparent by refusing to let him be his own person. Frequently, a stepchild has strong expectations about a new stepparent, hoping that he or she will be much like their absent biological parent, having the same personality, likes, tastes, character, temperament, and attitudes. One boy we worked with manifested great disappointment because his stepfather was not interested in baseball like his own father. The boy brooded about this and refused to have much to do with his stepdad because of it.

The stepchild may also hope to be treated the same way by the stepparent as by the natural parent. When this doesn't happen, disappointment and trouble may be around the corner.

The child is basically denying the personhood of the new parent. This makes it extremely difficult for the stepparent to be accepted for what he or she really is.

"I'm Laughing on the Outside but Crying on the Inside"

When a child uses denial, it is often difficult to detect his true thoughts and emotions. Children who may be really hurting may deny it by constantly saying, "It doesn't bother me." But those of us who counsel such youth know that they may be "laughing on the outside but crying on the inside."

Such denials can make it very tough to work with stepchildren, and some effort has to be made to help them realize what they are doing. By not admitting to their problems, they cannot take proper steps to resolve them. This is unhealthy and hurts themselves and the stepfamily.

"Who, Me, Upset?"

As we saw in the last chapter, one very grave psychological problem for a child is unresolved mourning over the loss of a parent through divorce or death. It can be so painful for the child that he may just pretend that his grief does not exist. As in repression, the stepchild may also deny angry feelings over the breakup of his parents and when made aware of it, will often be afraid to express the hostility.

The strength of this defense is very powerful in children because it is easy to do. How simple? Just "make believe" that your hurt doesn't exist. If you're not emotionally prepared to deal with a situation, then run away from it as fast as you can by denying it. No wonder it is so attractive to children and one of the most commonly utilized defenses.[1]

Let's face it. The feelings brought about by the separation of parents and the initiation into a stepfamily do stir up a lot of emotion. The easiest thing for the stepchild is to deny much feeling about it at all. "Who me? Upset, sad? Not me, it's their life. They can mess it up all they want," said one boy, when commenting about his newly blended family during counseling. Yet, he cried intermittently for days at home.

"I'll Lie My Way Out of It"

The behavior pattern of lying is the epitome of the denial defense. In this case the obvious aim of the stepchild, or anyone else for that matter, is to either make another person believe something that is not true or to disbelieve something that is.

But there may be a deeper, hidden meaning behind lying. Unconsciously, the child may actually be trying to deceive himself as well as others. In this way he actually distorts his own mind by not seeing the way life really is.

Stepparents have reported to us in counseling that a child who was once quite honest became a liar when his family life was threatened by divorce or remarriage. Of course, one of the tragedies of this aspect of denial is that when it is repeated over and over again, the child is sealed off from the truth and himself. He can actually, in time, believe his own lies and can get to the place where he is unable to separate truth from falsehood. Such is the main characteristic of pathological lying.

"I Just Don't Believe My Dad Was That Bad"

Children have a basic innate love for their natural parents and will often refuse to believe anything really bad about either parent. One of the knottiest problems and sorest points in stepfamilies is knowing what to tell children about the divorce and the absent parent.

For example, if the absent parent was largely responsible for the breaking up of the marriage, do you tell the child? Should the custodial or stepparent always make the absent parent look good? These are serious questions.

Denial of the facts is strongly tied into one of the most vital needs of stepchildren. That is the need to keep the absent parent *good* regardless of his behavior. Nearly all stepchildren we've encountered have this need for "idealization" of the missing parent. They do so with intense yearning to continue to maintain contact. For example, to compensate for the father's weaknesses some stepchildren fantasize him as the "biggest and the greatest." This shows how extreme the idealizing of the missing parent can become.

It galls many custodial parents that under the most glaring evidence of bad behavior, their child won't accept the facts about their absent parent. Many children resent hearing about the absent parent's alcoholism or sexual promiscuity that may have led to the divorce. The question is: Should the child be reminded about the deficiencies in that other person? Or, should the child be protected, knowing that a part of his identity lies with the other parent too? This is not an easy issue to deal with, and professionals are divided on the subject.

Should the custodial or stepparent always protect the absent parent?

We think not. By withholding information at times, the parent can actually perpetuate the denial mechanism in their children. If the absent parent evidences deep neurotic or psychotic manifestations, you may have a real problem on your hands.

Remember that children are not completely capable of sorting out the facts and may develop extremely strong attachments to the "ill" parent. By virtue of this strong bond there is always the risk of a deep emotional identification with the person and the accompanying "sick" patterns of behavior or attitudes.

If this problem exists in your family, you must bear in mind that the issue becomes complicated when a child is prohibited from seeing such an absent parent. We've found that not allowing the child to see that parent usually does not weaken, but strengthens, the relationship. This happens because the child may develop a very strong bond or protective mechanism out of pity for that parent.

We frequently run across parents who attempt to keep their children away from the ex-spouse for various reasons. But this strategy often backfires because of the child's intense need to keep the parents "good." Prohibiting visitation in some cases only increases the identification with the "ill" parent. It is better that a stepchild operate from a truth base than be restricted from seeing a parent—unless his life is in danger.

What constitutes an "ill" parent? How do we "tell it like it is" so a stepchild will be less apt to deny the truth when there are severe character defects?

The typical opinion found in Christian or non-Christian circles is that the responsibility for divorce should be shared equally by both parties. Even where adultery may have broken up a marriage, we have heard, "Well, I wonder what she did to drive him to another woman?" Or, "Hmm—she must have done something wrong or he never would have done it."

What's happened to the timeless biblical principles of accountability for the rightness and wrongness of one's actions? To sweep them under the rug in the name of marriage is to be inconsistent with God's standards, for He abhors wrongdoing.

Marriage is not above scrutiny, and it becomes more holy and less tarnished when God's standards are upheld. When truth is its guide, it becomes the state God intended it to be. Without a higher standard it loses its integrity.

We believe that God permits and expects us to use the discerning judgment of His Word in regard to marriage when it is needed. The words of Jesus "thou shalt not judge" are often misunderstood. He was referring to motives, not actions. If His words meant that no judgment whatsoever can be rendered, then we have a contradiction in the Bible when it says that we have the right to reprove, rebuke, and correct those who depart from God's standards for proper behavior (2 Timothy 3:16).

There are many situations where one of the spouses is innocent except for making a poor choice of marital partner. This is a key issue and has direct bearing on stepfamilies that have to deal with accountability, responsibility, and blame. It has to be dealt with because such questions are almost always raised in the stepfamily.

Is there no blame or lack of accountability in the first marriage

... if a man repeatedly beats his wife?

... if a woman has adulterous affairs?

... if a man has incestuous relationships?

... if an alcoholic endangers the lives of those around him?

... if a person is involved in drug abuse and threatens life?

... if a deeply immoral parent flaunts his sexual hang-ups through pornography?

It should also be noted that divorce is often actively sought by the ill parent for reasons that seem to reflect that person's disturbed thinking rather than any severe difficulties within the marriage itself.

We are not trying to say that one spouse is always perfect. What we are saying is that there are many cases where one spouse is acting so negatively or in such a deviant manner that he is destroying the marriage. And, in spite of all the efforts made by the other party, there is no way to continue with the marriage.

We realize many people may disagree with our position, including many Christians who believe you should stick it out no matter what. Nevertheless, we believe our position is valid.

Children, we might add, appear to be more damaged by a mother's disloyalty to the marriage bond than the father's. It comes back to the idea that the home centers on the mother, for children usually have a closer bonding to her.

From shaky foundations many a new stepfamily has to rebuild and try to deal with a disastrous past. This makes it critical for the step-child because, as we've stated earlier, he's going to (1) wonder what caused the divorce of his parents and (2) have the natural tendency to deny bad behavior in a parent.

These heavy issues are very difficult to deal with and many step-families have problems over them on a continuing basis even though they may not be openly discussed very often. We believe that if a step-child is not shown the wrong in people, his sense of justice will be im-paired as an adult and he may lose faith in the Bible, people, and the sanctity of marriage.

Stepchildren need to learn accountability and one of the best ways is to see its application in their own parents. Shielding a child from truth only diffuses and weakens his growing conscience. Exposing truth, fur-thermore, relieves the child of guilt if he believes he was partly re-sponsible for the divorce of his parents.

If you are faced with this tremendous problem in your stepfamily, we urge you to give strong consideration to what we have set forth.

"I'm Afraid I Might Turn Out Like My Parent"

We once counseled a brokenhearted, sixteen-year-old teenager named Jennifer. She approached us with tears in her eyes. We won-dered how this sweet girl could be so upset. During the very first ses-sion she looked at our faces searchingly as she confessed her great fear.

"What's troubling you so much, Jennifer?" we asked.

In a burst of tears she responded, "I'm afraid I'm going to turn out just like my mother."

"What do you mean?"

"Well, my mother has had a lot of affairs and several broken mar-riages, and she is now living with a man with whom she argues con-stantly, and I hear her lying to him all the time. I'm wondering if I am like her. I've cried myself to sleep many nights thinking about this. It's got me worried. Will I turn out the same way?"

You see, many children have this concern. If their parent is living an immoral life, they fear they might be like that parent. Their natural inclination is to think, *There also might be something wrong with me.*

Many stepchildren really do believe that they have inherited a parent's faults. This is one major reason stepchildren will deny the truth about a parent. So the denial defense gets tied up with the child's own self-esteem.

This leads us quite naturally into the consideration of several guidelines to help you if your child might be using the denial defense.

What Parents Can Do

Guideline #1—You don't always have to protect the absent parent when your child's self-esteem is at stake.

In the previous section we gave a strong argument for exposing any severe wrongdoing of an absent parent. Now, you should ask yourself, "Just what will this do to my child's self-image?" For example, "How will my child take it if I expose his father as an alcoholic?" Parents who are drug addicts, serve time in jail, are sexually loose, have been in a mental hospital or intensive psychotherapy, are plainly irresponsible, or just noncaring in their actions do present a tremendous challenge for the custodial parents.

In approaching the problem, one professional view is that you tell children only the bare minimum facts. Say very little, and if you do, render no personal insults or judgments. This way it helps the child to "save face." Then he won't have the tendency to believe there might be something woefully wrong with him too.

The other view accepts the idea that children need a truth base. We accept the idea that it is usually best to tell stepchildren the *basic* reasons underlying the divorce. It is surprising how frequently information is withheld that would have greatly relieved the hurts as well as guilt. As we stated earlier, children have the tendency to blame themselves—possibly an even greater blow to self-esteem.

If you give your children no truth base, the deceit will be harmful and may backfire. Their worst thoughts can neither be confirmed nor refuted. We have seen adults in counseling who grew up in a step-family without knowing the facts about their parents' breakup. This led to much anxiety. Uncertainty about one or both of their parents seemed to lay the groundwork for rootlessness that led to great insecurity and anxiety. Nearly all report that they would have liked much more information even if it were negative.

As a general guideline for this sticky problem, we'd suggest you be open, honest, and sensitive to what the child at the moment might be able to bear and help your child to accept the facts surrounding your divorce and ex-spouse. Then, as the child grows up, he has the freedom to decide, based on the truth, what kind of relationship he will have with the absent parent.

It is our opinion that the major burden of disclosing any truths about the absent parent and helping to develop proper attitudes in the child falls squarely on the shoulders of the custodial, natural parent—not the stepparent.

Guideline #2—*Don't deny contact with the absent parent.*

Do not prevent your child from seeing the absent parent unless it is absolutely necessary. Nearly all professionals agree on this. The only exception might be where physical or severe psychological damage might occur. Otherwise, if contact is blocked, emotional damage might result, because there is a universal urge to find and know one's roots.

Contact with the absent parent helps a child to face reality about that person. Then the child sees for herself what is going on and can in most cases then make the necessary adjustments.

Although the main burden of dealing with the disclosures surrounding a divorce belong to the natural parent, that parent and child are often dependent upon a stepparent's tact and understanding to avoid further hurt. The stepparent's cooperation in helping the children see their other natural parent can go a long way to avoid tension. Such emotional support can be extremely uplifting and helpful.

Virginia Satir makes this telling point for stepparents when she says:

Make room in your own mind for the stepchild's other parent. He is there. You can't wish him away. Remember, again, you need to win the child's trust. Give him plenty of opportunities to let him know that you are not trying to replace his other parent.[2]

Guideline #3—*Don't teach denial by rejecting feelings.*

It is not very wise to tell a child that he should not feel such and such. To get a person to deny his real feelings is risky business. He may come to the point that he denies his right to feel or to express them at all.

Parents can actually teach their children denial. They do this in one of two ways: (1) refusal to listen to the child's hurts and frustrations about family conditions (the child interprets this indirect message to mean that his feelings are not really important) and (2) through direct statements such as "You shouldn't feel that way" or "Aren't you going to grow up?" (this may teach a child that it is better to conceal his ideas and feelings).

Underneath, of course, the child fears rejection and loss if he does reveal his true self. When a person feels discounted for his feelings, he loses a sense of his own authenticity. Denial is the next step—both of himself and others.

In addition, you must help the stepchild realize that unpleasant situations or problems do not go away just because we don't think about them. If we work gently and lovingly, we can in time help them to realize that denying facts or feelings only compounds the problems later on.

Guideline #4—*Ease into the newness of the stepfamily.*

It might not be best, at first, to remove a child's denial mechanism, especially if they are quite young. It may be one of the best ways for them to cope with their fears and hurts. Wait until the child is ready to handle truth and develops trust in the parents who are primarily responsible for his care.

It should be understood that in most cases, however, denial is not best, for it may block healthy adjustment. We'd suggest going slowly at first and allowing the child time to find security in his custodial parents. A word now and then will suffice, and you must be delicate in the way you handle certain situations. Remember that when a stepchild is confronted about distortions, he may more adamantly hold on to them.

Guideline #5—Consider sound biblical advice.

The Bible indicates the importance of man's knowledge about truth and falsehood. Although the stepfamily is not expressly singled out, there is one biblical principle that would apply to all areas of life. Jesus gave us great insight when he said, "You shall know the truth, and the truth shall make you free" (John 8:32). This not only applies to Christ, who is Truth, but to life itself. Truth, not denial, ultimately makes one free, because when it is known, the person can make the necessary adjustments to live with it. When facts are denied, a person cannot understand his environment or himself.

Questions That Need Answering

1. Could my children be using the denial defense?
2. Am I perpetuating denial in my child by refusing to accept his feelings?
3. In my present situation is it best to withhold information or speak the whole truth?
4. Do I consider my child's self-esteem when I talk about our broken family?
5. Am I teaching my stepchildren to lie, through my own silence?
6. What is the best way to tell my child about his other parent outside our home?
7. Will my stepchild be better or worse for knowing the truth about the family?

5

"Why Does Tommy Act So Different?"

Many stepchildren literally change their behavior
by acting in a manner opposite from their usual
way. By using a *reaction formation,* they try to rub
out the past—which is very confusing to parents.

"I don't care if I live anymore. My real mother died two years ago
and since then everything has fallen apart. My parents are making me
go on to high school, but it ain't too swift anymore. Why should I?
School's a real drag—studying stuff I'll never use. Besides, every day is
an ordeal."

"Why's that?" we asked Bill, who wistfully looked toward the floor.

"Well, my stepmother is on my case all the time, and my father is no
better. I can't please them. At school the teachers bug me. It seems that
I can't do anything right." Bill began to choke up at this point in his
very first counseling session.

"Bill, when you're ready to talk, I'd like to know what's behind
those tears."

"Well, I've never told anyone this, but you seem to care. My mother
was my whole world. There wasn't a thing that she could not tell me
and vice versa. She gave me goals to live for and constantly told me
how great I was going to be someday. While she was well, I had drive
to do things and was a leader in my class at school and Boy Scouts.
Now, who cares? Dad doesn't pay much attention. He's too goo-goo

eyed over Virginia, my stepmom, and he's so into his career it makes me sick. Boy, it just hurts that Mom's gone, that's all."

After a long pause, I said, "Tell me more about your stepmother. You seem very upset with her. Could that be true?"

"My stepmom? She's a poor second. She tries, I guess, but honestly she gives me the impression that I'm extra baggage around home. And, one thing I hate about her is that she always steps between Dad and me. If he and I argue, she tells me to get out and leave him alone because he's tired. If we have plans, she seems always to butt in and try to prevent us from going together."

"Time is about up, but Bill, you and I need to talk more about your feelings toward your mother and stepmom. Before you go I have one last question. Have you changed much since your mother's death?"

"Strange, Doc, that you should ask that because quite a few friends have told me they see a great change. And, I can see that I'm not the same. I used to be open about things and very forward. Nothing got to me. I guess now I've become pretty tame. I even walk away from fights, which I never used to do. Now, too, I'm not interested in any sports teams. But the worst is, I don't care anymore."

Bill's behavior is a good example of what we professional counselors call a *reaction formation*. In simple terms he was behaving or acting in an extreme manner that was very untypical. In fact, his father later commented that his behavior had been so bizarre that he wondered if his boy could posssibly have some kind of split personality.

During counseling one of the projective personality tests given this fourteen-year-old youth revealed that he was almost ready to give up on life. He dreaded the future because he felt trapped and saw no promise of hope. Having lost the ability to fight back, assert himself, and express his individuality, he became extremely passive. The result was a very weak self-esteem. He confessed that he had numerous thoughts about taking his own life.

This created tension for his father and stepmother, too, because Bill seldom shared his true inner feelings about anything. This created problems with his stepmother especially. She angrily stated that she never knew where she stood with him. Yet, he would go on misbehaving. But when confronted about it, he'd only pout and turn into a very submissive person, the very opposite of his real personality.

This acting opposite is a form of repression because a person is usually unaware of the change. You've heard the saying: Our minds play tricks on us. The reaction-formation defense truly falls into this category. If threatening thoughts or feelings begin to enter the conscious mind, we may try to keep them repressed by either overreacting or acting the opposite of what we truly feel.

In Bill's case, when his hostile feelings were aroused, he sought to present another image of himself. He became docile and extremely passive around the house, but he nearly always hid his true feelings about his deceased mother and his stepmother. In this way he sought to protect himself against the trauma of whatever had happened to him. This is very common, but it does not mean that every time your stepchild acts different he's in a reaction formation. Everyone uses reaction formation at certain times as a way of coping with problems and stress. But if the new behavior persists over a long period of time, then it might be that this defense is being used as a way of avoiding conflict.

What Was Bill Doing?

Bill sought a substitute that was far removed and little resembled the original feelings of hurt. The aim of reaction formation then is to counter the original feelings. When a person accomplishes this goal, he has actually adopted an attitude that contradicts the original one.

People, therefore, can conceal hate with a facade of love, or cruelty with kindness. The new feelings or attitudes help to keep the real but dangerous desires from entering the consciousness or from being carried out in action.

This makes reaction formations very subtle. Further illustrations in true life can give us a better grasp of this illusive, but yet interesting, defense. A reaction formation may be manifested by those who crusade militantly against loose sexual morals or the evils of alcohol. Sometimes those people have a background of earlier difficulties with such problems themselves, and their zealous crusading appears to be a reaction that safeguards them against a recurrence of such feared behavior.

Or consider the person who is an avowed pacifist. He may have constant feelings of hostility or aggression. When he becomes intense about promulgating peace at any price, he does not have to deal with his underlying feelings of hatred.

How a Stepfather Reacted

While counseling people in stepfamilies, we see the reaction-formation defense at work in several ways. When those same individuals get insight into how they are using a reaction formation, it gives them a tool to bring about a change in their behavior.

Ken was a sharp, conscientious man in his mid-thirties. When he remarried, he gained an instant family because his wife, Dottie, had three young children. Dottie called our office one day, just furious. She said she was ready to kick Ken out because of the overly strict rules and harsh punishment he laid down for the children. At times, she admitted, Ken could have broken some of her children's bones.

When her husband came in with her, at our request, for the next session, he began to open up about his past marriage and relationship to his own children. "I did a lousy job raising my kids," he confessed. "I was way too easy on them."

Ken began to see immediately when we suggested the possibility that he was reacting in an unconscious manner to the guilt he felt about being neglectful toward his own children. He could also see that he possibly was punishing himself by getting Dottie angry at him, because he felt unworthy as a father. We helped to point out that he was using a reaction formation to try to deal with those nagging feelings out of the past. He had a new awareness when he came to understand that harsh, punitive judgment on Dottie's children did not work to relieve his guilt over the original family. Furthermore, he saw that his harshness only denied him a warm and loving relationship with his stepchildren.

We're glad to add that Ken accepted the truth about himself very graciously, and he abruptly changed his attitudes and methods of punishment with his stepchildren. But this true story demonstrates how destructive the reaction-formation defense can become. Like the other defenses, it blinds us to the reality of why we think and behave the way we do, causing grief and heartache in the end.

In stepchildren this defense can be seen at work in various ways. One stepfamily we dealt with tried to have family powwows to get the feelings of each member out in the open. The experiment did not work because no one would talk and open up. It was then that they decided to have counseling in order to discuss the rules and needs within the family. The sessions began after school. The mother, a sister, and Rob attended the sessions. Up to this point, by his parents' admission, Rob had been a fairly quiet, cooperative boy—which also was manifested in counseling. It wasn't long until the boy, a junior-high student, began arriving late for the sessions. When he did arrive, he usually expressed great anger over the fact that his bike broke down or that he had to stay after school. We knew that he had a resistance to counseling, however, because his body language and nonverbal communication signals betrayed him.

This boy was using a reaction formation of quietness against being able to express his angry feelings about his family. Later, his anger was a reaction against being unable to express his real feelings about being in counseling. So, instead of projecting weakness, he portrayed a more surface emotion—namely, anger. He also was a "holy terror" in his school and social life. This anger circumvented his real feelings and for the moment enhanced his self-esteem.

It is very common for a child to act just the opposite of what normally would be expected. This is how he protects himself from trauma. Let's look at several typical instances where this defense might be used in a stepfamily.

"I'm Not Going to Take That From Anybody"

Defiance is another very common form of this defense. You will want to take note of this because impudence in stepchildren is often a reaction formation that helps to muster up courage as a defense against the fear of being punished or a sudden rush of love for a stepparent. Defiance, then, in the stepchild acts as a blocking mechanism to cover up the real feelings.

The opposite of being defiant is to be passive. One tall, lanky teenager named Phil would never enter into the conflicts in his stepfamily. Whenever a discussion would come up dealing with those conflicts, he'd always find some excuse so he wouldn't have to talk about them. When he began to unfold the story about his family life when growing up, you could see how he was presently reacting to the past. His passivity had virtually become a reaction formation.

Here's his story: "I remember that I used to hate being at home. My parents could never understand why I was always down at a friend's house. I hated family get-togethers. I didn't even like to be in family pictures. My mother and father couldn't even have their pictures taken without some big hassle. I can still see the rages of my mother. One time she threw a hot iron across the room at my sister. And, I can still see my father in a terrible rage knocking down the Christmas tree on Christmas Eve because he was mad about some stupid little thing. My home was filled with constant tension. I could never predict what kind of a mood everybody would be in when I came home.

"I just got so sick of it that I said to myself many times, while thinking about where my life was going, that when I grow up there won't be any anger in my home. I'll just play it cool and try to keep an even temper at all times."

What Phil had done was to transfer his upset about tension right into the stepfamily—long before he had grown up. He simply refused to get involved in confronting situations, so he developed a reaction against the anger in his past. If he doesn't break this pattern in himself, we're afraid that Phil may have a very troubled marriage. And it's all because he went to the extreme. He had never learned in his original family how to handle conflict. Instead, his attitude taught him to run.

This illustration teaches us the awesome truth that reaction formations can affect a person for years. As a matter of fact, if they are constantly used, they may become a permanent part of one's behavior pattern.

"Why Don't They Yell at My Stepsister?"

When two original families with children are blended together, constant fighting and friction among the children are very common. Abrupt changes in children often occur. It's bad enough in the biological family where there is normal sibling rivalry. In the stepfamily this seems to be much more pronounced. An angry stepchild, who is feeling hurt or abandoned, might turn to intimidation to get his point across, whereas before he may have been a very docile child.

Connie, one such ten-year-old, told us this story after relating that she didn't get along very well with her new stepmother's daughter. "I can't do anything right. My stepmother always buys Leslie things and not me. It doesn't seem fair. She can eat and drink in the living room, but I'm not allowed to do those things. I get very mad so I fight with Leslie. When I do, I'm the only one who gets yelled at."

In talking with Connie's father and stepmother we discovered that she was very mean and hateful toward her stepsister. Connie's father indicated that she had always been a very quiet child. She never sassed or talked back. He said that she was extremely compliant and never misbehaved. He also sadly stated that his daughter had become a monster almost overnight. "I just can't believe how Connie has changed. She fights all the time with her sister. Worse than that, she seems to go out of her way to stir up trouble."

Intimidation of brothers and sisters by stepchildren may be a reaction formation. The passive stepchild can suddenly become aggressive because he is anxious and very afraid.

If a child like Connie feels defeated and unable to gain any control over those people and events in life that have brought frustration and havoc, she might very well take things into her own hands as a reaction against the deeper feelings of helplessness.

"I Never Get Any Breaks"

A key reaction-formation pattern or mental attitude that we often see in our counseling is the "poor me" syndrome. We find this most frequently in stepchildren. They go around much of the time feeling sorry for themselves. It is important to know that people who wallow in self-pity actually feel a great deal of self-contempt because they cannot solve their problems. They will soak in their self-pity to protect themselves from the highly threatening emotion of self-hate by adopting the opposite viewpoint. They see themselves in need of sympathy and consolation instead.

Self-pity is actually a state of mind where a person believes he can't solve or change his problems. This is what produces the feelings of self-contempt and helplessness. Unable to accept that about themselves, the individual uses self-pity as an emotional cover-up.

Stepchildren often find themselves in a world of trying to survive. Believing there is little they can do to help themselves, they'll use the "poor me" attitude, trying to tell themselves they really do deserve sympathy and support because they are so helpless about changing their plight.

Self-pity is, therefore, a reaction against the deeper feelings of anger. Unfortunately, the temporary feelings of pity block the person from seeing the true self because he continues to avoid change and decisions to turn his life around. Resolution, therefore, is impossible until he refuses any longer to soak in his "pity parties." Self-pity is irrational. It never gets anyone anywhere.

"I'm the Greatest"

Another frequently used pattern is the "Gee, I'm just great" syndrome. We call this self-glory. This type of reaction formation, like self-pity, is another defensive means to alleviate painful feelings of self-contempt. Self-glory creates the belief that some glorious success is just around the corner. It can become insatiable and blinds the person to reality.

Self-glory is found in both the stepparent and stepchild. A stepmother, for example, may fill her mind with fanciful expectations that she is going to take care of the whole situation as she becomes a part of a new family that is hurting. With this kind of thinking she will often set herself up for heartache. When she begins to fail to reach her expectations, she will then avoid punishing herself for trying by acting like the perfect mother, which of course she cannot be.

In the stepchild self-glory can be manifested by the "bully" syndrome. With low self-esteem and lacking confidence, the big bully has to "shoot off his mouth" to make everybody think he's the toughest or the greatest. In reality, he doesn't feel that way at all. But he creates a reaction formation to prove to himself and others that he is strong and powerful. He can't face admitting to anything else.

Self-glory, like self-pity, conceals feelings of self-hate and weakness because the adult or child can't change the helpless condition in which he finds himself. This makes the sufferer believe himself to be all-powerful and very capable. Believing this, the person may be paralyzed as far as gaining insight into his real self and the self-defeating behavior he manifests. Change is thus blocked because the person won't face the truth that he has trouble coping with certain aspects of life. He will go on in his fantasy that all is well even though his life may be falling apart. Self-glory is fruitless since it leads to self-deception and only works for a time. As parents come to understand self-pity and self-glory, they can move to help a child to understand himself better.

Subtle Clues

In a stepchild these defensive patterns are not so easily discernible. There are certain clues to watch for, however. The "poor me" attitude just discussed is often used to obtain attention or sympathy. The child may take on a passive role to get what he wants. Underneath is hurt or anger. As against the strong aggressive feelings that the child is afraid to disclose, he may turn inward and try to get a reaction in another way.

Self-glory or the "Gee, I'm great" attitude is nearly always a concealment of anger turned toward the self. When a child in a stepfamily who was quiet and humble begins to manifest a boastful, know-it-all attitude, it may be a strong clue that he is reacting to something that lies beneath the surface.

A seventeen-year-old youth named Jack illustrates well this syndrome. After a couple of months in counseling his thoughts shot backward in time as he thought of his dead mother. Watching his father yell at his stepmother often brought the past to the present as he reflected about how his father had treated his mother the same way. These thoughts were expressed several times during the course of his counseling.

Jack was thirteen when his mother died. He had always had a good relationship with her, and they were very close. He was a quiet and thoughtful boy. He did well in school, had made good friends, and was very active in his church group. His best friend was the pastor's son.

Over a period of several months Jack began to change. His father and new stepmother were extremely upset. That's how he got into counseling. We were told by his parents that at the age of seventeen his outlook as well as behavior had greatly changed. While talking to Jack, it came to light that he was sure his present behavior would have upset his mother quite a bit.

He was surly, disrespectful, and overbearing, and no one could give him any advice. His friends were part of a very fast crowd, and he hadn't attended church in over two years. His passive nature had turned to one of rage. His main target was his father and anyone in earshot. He often thought: "If only I had protected my mother more from the rotten temper of my father, maybe she would still be alive today." Hysterically, she had left home one night in tears over a big fight with his dad. She died from injuries sustained when her car hit a tree head-on.

As we began to zero in on the "new and different" Jack with his anger and know-it-all attitude, he was even surprised at himself that his feelings were vented in such force. While Jack's real mother was alive, he was very passive and submissive. After she died, he blamed himself. So his aggressiveness after his father had remarried was really a reaction against the bad feelings he had for not stepping in between his father and mother when he was younger. He was really angry at himself, so the anger was externalized and his passive nature turned into one of rage.

When Jack himself came to understand why and what he was doing, he was able to redirect his negative behavior and bad attitude by boxing at a local gym. He slowly pulled himself together, and the last we heard he was involved in his church again and had completed two semesters of college. He was much happier.

What Parents Can Do

Guideline #1—Watch for mood changes or when a child, over a period of time, does not seem to be "himself."

A stepchild who does change from one extreme to another may need to be watched. As we saw in Rob, a child who has literally been a "holy terror" and suddenly becomes totally passive is probably trying to deal with emotions that lie beneath the surface. Actually the stepchild could be lapsing into a deep emotionally disturbed state or even some mental illness.

Guideline #2—Reinforce caring attitudes.

Always expect, at least at first, that a stepchild is harboring some hurts carried over from the past. Extra care and sensitivity is vital in helping to prevent children from dealing with those negative feelings and hurts in an extreme manner, such as reaction formation. Stepparents should do everything they can to let their stepchildren know that they love them and accept them.

Such an approach will help the child to relax when he knows that both the natural and stepparent will always be there when needed. In this way the child comes to realize that he has little to fear and that there is no need to overreact or to gain attention in unhealthy ways.

Guideline #3—Talk with your stepchildren about healthy ways to cope with their hurts from the past.

It will be of great help to your child if you can help him see why he is reacting in such a way if he has gone to extremes. You might want to say something like this:

"John, we've been noticing some changes in you. We wonder if you are even aware of what you're doing or thinking? Could it be possible that you are hurting or upset over (name several possibilities)? Can you see that you may be overreacting now as a way of dealing with a past problem or hurt?"

These are some of the questions you might ask in order to help your child come to better understand himself. You can help him to see that acting in an extreme way is very deceptive because he's covering up his true feelings. You might add such words as: "John, you have got to take a good hard look at yourself before you can face your real problems."

If they are old enough to comprehend what you are saying, it is important to talk to your stepchildren about this defense if you suspect they are using it to avoid real feelings.

Guideline #4—Correct the "poor me" attitude.

If your stepchild talks constantly about how bad things are or discloses self-pity, be aware that he is searching for attention of some kind to elevate his self-esteem. Try verbally to bolster his self-confidence, and above all let him know that he can change his life to a great extent and go on to achieve. By having his ego or self-esteem reinforced, the child won't have to react in an extreme manner to deal with his problems.

Guideline #5—Consider sound biblical advice.

King Solomon, centuries ago, showed us in capsule form the effect that emotions have on our lives, when he said: "A joyful heart makes a cheerful face, but when the heart is sad, the spirit is broken" (Proverbs 15:13).

When a person's spirit is broken, he may often go to any length to relieve the pain. It is good to help stepchildren face their hurts realistically and also to turn them to the Lord, who is able to set free the brokenhearted (*see* Luke 4:18).

Questions That Need Answering

1. Is my child acting in extreme ways? What are they?
2. Does my stepchild get caught up in a lot of self-pity?
3. Does my stepchild appear to overreact in inappropriate ways? How?
4. Do I ever notice that my child is playing a role and is acting in a completely different way than usual?
5. Does my stepchild manifest much self-contempt?
6. Does my child tend to intimidate the other children in our family? How?
7. Do I keep in mind that many a broken spirit has been healed by the tenderness of a smile?

III

The Stepchild Who Just Goes Along Passively

Stepchildren who seem to remain on the fringe of family involvement can be very exasperating to parents. This pattern is called *accommodation*. In the next three chapters we will cover three additional psychological defenses, which show a child's compliance in a typical stepfamily. They are *rationalization, isolation,* and *fantasy formation*. These terms can readily be understood by the parent who may have questions such as:

1. Why does my child appear to have few feelings?
2. Why does my child choose to be a loner?
3. Why does my child seem to choose the "dream world" rather than logical reasoning?

6

"I'll Logically Explain Away My Problems"

Who hasn't tried to explain things away by *rationalizing?* The stepchild is no exception, because it is a way to avoid frustration and hurtful feelings by using thought alone.

"Why do my children want to see their father? He is almost everything a father shouldn't be, and they have such a wonderful stepfather to take care of them now. Last night my daughters received a phone call out of the blue. It was their father. He called to let them know that he had just remarried. By the way, this is his fourth marriage, and he hasn't even reached middle age. They seemed excited when the call came, but when they hung up they expressed disappointment," explained the exasperated mother in our office.

"In the past he has consistently been inconsistent. He's been back and forth—in and out of their lives so many times I've lost count. He breaks promises to see them. He says he'll buy them things and then fails to produce. His child support has been very erratic, so they can never depend on it for clothes, school functions, or youth activities at church that require money. He's transient in his jobs, is an alcoholic, and smokes pot regularly. One of his ex-wives even tried to get the girls to smoke pot and drink before they were teenagers.

"Their dad constantly tears down good values, morals, and the church, which has come to mean so much to them. He also seethes with hate and deceit and blows up at them because of their loyalty to our home. There have been occasions when I or my husband have had to grab the phone because they have become so upset with him," she continued.

"My girls have even admitted that he embarrasses them in front of their friends. So, why do they want a relationship with him? They have openly stated to us that they hate him, never want to see him again, but this all seems to change with one phone call or contact. Should we let them continue to see him? My mother, family, and friends wonder and ask me why they want to see their father, and I really wonder the same. Why?"

We explained to this puzzled mother that children nearly always try to justify the behavior of the natural parent and keep hoping to get that parent back. We told her that we needed to talk with her daughters in order to understand the situation better.

The following week Brenda and Ann came for a counseling session. They were pleasant and friendly and didn't mind talking about themselves. We broke in, "Your mother told us that you girls have had many problems with your father since you were very small."

Ann answered, "That's just the way he is, and he's not so bad."

"I can handle being around him a short while," Brenda added.

After a lull in the conversation, we asked a searching question. "How does it feel to have your father marry again and have a new stepmother."

Brenda offered, "Well, maybe this time it's going to work. He can't help the way he is, because he had such a bad childhood."

Ann backed up her sister, "I don't mind the way Dad is. I know he lies and he breaks promises, and I have cried a lot because of it, but it doesn't matter. He tries and I just think about the good times we have together and forget the rest. Besides, he told me he's going to buy me a car and pay my way through college. He'd even send me to Europe if I'd ask. He has a hard time showing us he loves us, but he's so busy he doesn't have the time. He can't help it."

Talk about rationalizations! Even though his track record spoke for itself, the girls wanted so much to believe that their father loves them they just accepted his grandiosity and inconsistencies, knowing that he couldn't deliver. In addition, they explained away his maladaptive behavior by creating excuses for him.

Take another true illustration that shows how rationalization can lead toward poor decisions that may affect a stepchild, or any child for that matter, for years to come.

Diane, Dwayne's daughter, had come to live with him and his wife, Jo, two months before, after she ran away from her mother's house. Diane had stated at that time that she wanted to change and get away from the immoral, hostile, and rigid life-style that her mother subjected her to. The girl said, "I've had it and I don't want to turn out like my mother."

Dwayne and his wife had taken Diane in and tried to make a good home for her, but she balked at the closeness and the kindness extended toward her, especially by her stepmother. Although they didn't realize it at the time, Diane had been taking drugs and misbehaving in school while she was living with them. After Diane had been with them for a short time, she announced that she wanted to return home to her mother. With sadness and confusion Dwayne returned Diane to her mother.

A short time later, Dwayne called to say: "I don't know what to do with my daughter. She just told me that she and her mother are at it again. They just had a fistfight in front of their home for all the neighbors to see. Now she has run away again and called me from a phone booth saying, 'I'm not going back to Mom's house again to live.'

"Two weeks ago when I took her to her mother's house she said she no longer wanted to live with us here. She hated the school and the neighborhood. Those were only excuses. I think she felt obligated to go back to take care of her mother. 'I can help her to change,' was the way she put it. Why does she continue to go back to that hostile environment, and why doesn't she want to live in our home where we don't scream and beat each other up? We practice common courtesy. We don't have a violent home. Why would Diane jeopardize her future happiness and opportunity to learn what a decent, responsible, and successful life could be like instead of living with such a loser as her mother? Diane thinks she can change her mother and make her into a good person. Is there something wrong with her thinking this way?" Dwayne asked.

"There's plenty wrong," we told him. "That's the 'I can change the situation' rationalization."

In both of these stories we can see the tremendous power and hold rationalization can have on people—stepchildren in particular. In the first, rationalization had led Brenda and Ann to accept their father's behavior. In the second, Diane had decided to go back again to live with her real mother because she foolishly thought that she could change and protect her.

What Was Wrong With These Girls?

It's interesting that in both stories the girls had "psyched themselves up" so the pain wouldn't be so bad. The stories also reinforce the fact that children never do give up on their natural parents. We've seen this time and time again.

Rationalization is a major defense and is common to us all. In stepchildren, especially, it is a means to actually suppress the emotional aspect of very hurtful situations. Through the intellect they develop a counterattack against feared emotions. Often this defense is very difficult to detect because rationalizations do often contain an element of truth.

There are many illustrations of this defense. The following show how rationalizations work.

A student may not want to study. He decides to go to a ball game instead. He knows he should study, so he comes up with various excuses to justify his decision. "A fella has to have some fun sometime." "We only live once." "Relaxation will clean out the cobwebs to help me study later."

A person may justify cheating on exams by pointing out that everybody is doing it.

These examples show us how attitudes or feelings in a given situation become permissible when the mind justifies them as "reasonable." Such a defense actually deceives a person into believing shallow explanations to justify behavior that is unacceptable and even illicit—but it preserves self-esteem and reduces anxiety. In this way the person avoids the conflict of the original painful thoughts or frustrated desires. Rationalization may also be used to relieve guilt, failure, and disappointment caused by those frustrated desires. Intellectualizing and rationalizing are really one and the same thing.

Rationalization can be used to depersonalize an event by reacting to it purely on an intellectual level, so the person is insulated from his feelings. This helps a person to deny part of reality—his own emotions. Remember, too, there is often some truth in rationalization, because arguments that are too weak would be unlikely to stand. It is only upon closer inspection—a step the rationalizer is careful to avoid— that the logic breaks down. In the opening story of this chapter, Ann's comment about her father's being too busy to show her much love demonstrates this clearly. Although her father may well be busy, she would not want to pursue the matter too far for fear she may find out that he is not busy at all.

This defense would naturally be used by older stepchildren, say from eight or nine upward, because their thought processes are better formulated. It is easier for them to use abstract reasoning and thereby find excuses to explain what has happened to them. Let us now turn to some of the major or typical rationalizations we've discovered while working with stepchildren. There are many more.

"My Parents Will Get Back Together Again"

Stepchildren continually tell us that they not only hope but believe their parents will get back together again. This rationalization helps them cling to the idea that their parents' divorce is only temporary.

Even when a child is told the facts about the separation of his parents, and one or both have remarried, he may carry rationalizations about the absent parent's returning at any time. Stepchildren have been heard to say, "Mother has gone over to Grandmother's house but will be back soon." "Dad gets home every night after I'm in bed and leaves too early the next morning for me to see him." "When Dad is gone long enough, he'll be back."

As noted when discussing the denial defense, such thoughts are untrue but are maintained in order to deny the hurtful facts of the separation of the stepchild's parents.

No matter what defense the child may be using, parents must firmly but gently reinforce the permanency of the split and encourage the child to accept this reality.

"If Only Things Were Different"

Many stepparents complain of hearing this refrain all too often. One stepfather told us that his teenage boy constantly mumbled when he was disciplined or did not get his way, "I'd certainly be much happier if certain people weren't around here. It's ridiculous what we have to put up with now because Dad's gone."

Such thoughts can capture a child's thinking to the point that he can't, or won't, see any possible success in the new blended family or his own personal life. This generalized "isn't it awful" syndrome tends to put the blame on situations and conditions for his plight or unhappiness.

Two experts on stepfamilies explain that the "if only things were different" rationalization can be a stepchild's last-ditch effort to cope. It is quite true that if the stepchild's real parent were at hand, things would be different. In children's minds, this gets them off the hook, releasing them from their responsibility to deal with the situation.[1]

"If only things were different" is merely an idea that the world would be better "if." This idealization is closely related to the dream about the real parents getting back together again. As indicated earlier, children may tenaciously hold onto this belief for many years.

"It's Probably Better in the Other House"

There may be a lot of truth in this rationalization, but it's the old "grass is greener on the other side" notion that can often lead to disillusionment. There is not one of us who has not at one time or another had such a thought about some aspect of life. Many stepchildren live with this notion almost every hour of their waking time.

Because time with the noncustodial parent is limited, stepchildren will often dream about going to live with that parent, no matter what the situation might be. "Life has got to be better there than the way I have it" is the way one stepchild phrased it.

The problem with this notion is that it may blind the child to the virtues of his current home and the genuine and wholesome attitudes offered by the caring adults who live at home with him. Of course, living with the noncustodial parent for a time is more often than not the best medicine the doctor can prescribe. It's amazing how fast such a rationalization can be broken down when a child goes away to live for a while with that other parent. Of course, in some cases that other home might indeed be preferable. Just because a parent has custody does not mean that he or she is better equipped to meet the child's needs.

"Because I've Lost So Much, People Now Have to Take Care of Me"

This form of rationalization is what the psychologist calls a *claim* or entitlement. The use of this notion can drive parents crazy trying to meet all the demands placed on them by their children. This is the "you owe me a living" rationale. By rationalizing that because he has suffered so much and has sacrificed his dreams due to his real parents' mistakes, the stepchild believes that others should now take care of him.

Frequently, the stepparent and natural parent who have the custody are the ones who are expected to honor such a claim. They may be totally unaware of this rationalization in their child. If the child manifests a haughty attitude by expecting people to wait on him and snap to it at his every whim, it may be a clue that he is using the claim rationalization. Be aware, however, that your child is probably really hurting. Claims protect the sufferer from the threatening belief that nobody cares or will do anything to help.

"My Dad Can Beat Up Your Dad"

This is a very common statement heard on the school or neighborhood playground. All children seem to have a natural, inborn idea that their parents can do anything. This notion may even be exaggerated in a stepchild who is having difficulty in accepting the new family arrangement.

One stepfather came in to a session after his first Saturday picnic excursion with his new family. His stepson seemed to be very eager to learn about baseball. Charles, the new stepfather, was just as eager to get across certain skills to help the boy. Out of the blue the boy began making statements comparing him with his real dad. "My dad can hit the ball farther than you." "My dad says that is not the right way to catch the ball."

Charles, not prepared for such responses, overreacted with great hurt.

This rationalization is one of the ways a child deals with the absent parent. Kids cannot imagine that a parent does not love them, so they attempt to master the loss by giving their parents almost superhuman powers. You must remember that the child is trying to deal with loss and not necessarily putting you down.

"Well, I'm Unlovable Anyway"

Many a stepchild who gets caught up in a loyalty conflict over the absent parent who neglects him embraces this idea. This is especially so when that parent has constantly failed to be in regular contact. Even though the parent demonstrates insensitivity and lack of conscience in helping to support the child emotionally, the child will nearly always hold on to the idea that such a parent is not unloving or noncaring.

Such a stepchild will create all kinds of excuses as to why the parent doesn't call, write, or visit. One girl we worked with came in with several letters she had written but claimed her father had written. Her need to believe that he truly cared was so great that she didn't even bat an eye when confronted about the letters.

The stepchild who believes that his absent parent may have rejected him or does not love him will go to great lengths to try to explain this away. Unable to accept this belief, the child may rationalize: "Daddy would love me if I was lovable." This somehow lessens the sting of rejection as the child takes most of the blame upon himself.

"I'll Just Make It Tough on Everybody"

The problem of guilt created by loyalty conflicts frequently will make a stepchild invent reasons for not cooperating or getting along with the stepparent. Some stepchildren have actually admitted that if they can't control the situation, then they will subvert the blended family in some way. They don't use that term, but in essence that is precisely what they mean.

Such thoughts may not break out into open warfare or conflict but may turn up in thinking processes such as "Well, I've had such a raw deal, I don't owe it to anyone to work on relationships" or "I'll show everybody I won't be pushed around."

Many stepchildren are mighty successful in using this rationalization, as we shall see when we come to the discussion of the defense of displacement.

"I Can Blame Others for My Problems"

This rationalization is most common and at the same time very serious because a stepchild who thinks this way does so to relieve himself of some responsibility for making his new blended family work. He may also think this way to relieve any sense of lingering guilt he may feel for having some part in the breakup of his original home.

Children generally use this rationalization to their own great advantage. A stepchild can easily go overboard on this one. Witness this statement made to us by one child in counseling: "Everything that goes wrong with me now I can blame on my parents because they broke up my home." She went on to disclose the subtlety of this thinking process by blaming them for her stolen bike. It didn't matter that her parents' divorce took place two years before the bike was taken. When we reminded her that she was the one who left it unlocked, she reasoned, "Well it wouldn't have happened if Dad and Mom lived together because we would still be living in another town and on a different street. Besides, Dad fixed us girls a special stall for our bikes in a corner of the garage where they would be perfectly safe."

It is quite obvious what Gretchen was doing. We helped her during counseling to evaluate what she was doing and to correct this faulty thinking. She was not only afraid of being wrong and taking blame for anything but also was acting that way to bolster her self-esteem. We're glad to report that she learned to take personal blame for her faults and mistakes, and to find better ways to enhance her self-image and confidence.

In chapter ten, where we deal with *projection,* we'll talk about this rationalization in more depth. But what you've got to realize here is that if your stepchild starts blaming people for his own failures, he is using this defense to his own detriment, and the self-deception may influence him throughout life.

The above are just a few of the many ways rationalizations can pop up with stepchildren. Following are some guidelines for dealing with any faulty thinking in your children.

Guideline #1—Be aware that the rationalization defense is often cleverly disguised.

It is not always a simple matter to deal with this defense because it *is* so disguised. You will only know if your child has this problem by listening carefully to his conclusions or opinions on the issues and events that have influenced his life. If there are definite distortions of facts or conclusions based on weak evidence, then you might strongly consider that your child's thinking has become a defense.

This may mean some real work on your part to find out what your child is actually thinking. Gentle prodding is essential in trying to get the child to share his ideas.

Remember that stepchildren don't easily give up their self-protective rationalizations. You will, therefore, have to practice real patience in order to get a true picture of how your child is viewing things and whether he is making an adjustment to your new blended family.

Guideline #2—Be aware that your children may be harboring great sadness.

There is nearly always a note of sadness in stepchildren even though they may admit that the divorce of their parents might have been the very best thing. A teenage boy once said, "Intellectually, I understand all the reasons, but I don't like it. It makes me feel sick when I think about it. I thought when you fell in love it was for good. How could my parents be in love and then not be in love? Sometimes it hurts to think about it." This youth had some trouble talking about the reasons. But as he spoke, he eventually choked up, admitting he was very sad.

If your child conveys sadness when talking about the losses in his life, you need to develop a very sympathetic spirit. Sadness can block reasonable thinking. It might be best to help him through the emotional pain at the time. Later you can deal with what he is actually thinking. In other words, try to be sensitive to your child, always taking your cues from him in terms of how you should respond for the moment.

Guideline #3—Accept the fact that the natural, custodial parent needs to take the lead in getting at the rationalizations.

When helping stepchildren to change their thinking patterns, someone has to take the leadership role. This should fall upon the parent with whom the children will feel most at ease in talking. Usually, it is the natural parent. In time, this role can shift toward the stepparent when trust and a good relationship is established. At the same time, the natural parent needs to worry about protecting the child too much. You may overcome this by allowing freedom for the stepparent to eventually get involved in the process of deeper communication.

One stepmother expressed to her husband during a counseling session, "I just can't get close to your children unless you let me discuss their problems with them. I need to know what they are thinking, if they will tell me. When they pull back, I need to have the freedom to go to them and help them work out these problems." When this husband finally stopped protecting his children and allowed her this wish, tension in the home was drastically diminished.

But all in all, the natural parent is usually the one who must be aware of what the child is thinking and be the one to try to change any rationalizations.

Guideline #4—Attempt to change your stepchild's confused thinking when it is first expressed.

Stepchildren do have confused notions and ideas about their stepparent. They may indeed rationalize about such aspects of the stepparent's behavior as the way he disciplines. One boy put it this way, "My stepdad just loves to dish it out to me. I know he does. It's because he doesn't like me."

At times you've got to sit down with your child and help him face facts, by saying something like this: "Son, your stepdad isn't going to change. He disciplines you because he truly cares for you." Challenge your child to think through in a logical or reasonable way what you have just told him. For example, help him to understand that discipline is tied in with love: "If your stepdad didn't care, he'd just let you run the streets wild."

You could also challenge your child's thinking by asking questions that demand more than yes-and-no answers. For example, "Can you think of ways your stepfather's punishing of you shows you that he could truly care for you?" When helping your child face the real facts, don't openly express hurt at his *candid* comments, for example, when he may defend his other parent. He may be doing this either to get your reaction or to actually defend that person. Simply listen to those comments; let him share and give his opinions. You may be given a number of significant clues about what your child is thinking. Then you have something to work with. This may prepare the way for real honesty and truth down the road.

*Guideline #5—**Remember that your child holds the key, when you attempt to deal with his rationalizations.***

You need constantly to ask yourself, "How are my child's attitudes, thoughts, or ideas affecting his self-esteem and understanding of the truth?" If these attitudes, thoughts, or ideas render harm in some way to him and the stepfamily, you will want to discuss this with him carefully. He may be able to hold on to certain rationalizations in order to maintain his self-esteem, as long as these attitudes are not causing direct harm within your family. You may want to let him do this for a while, but always try to help him see the truth. If in time you don't seem to be getting through, then you may have to seek professional counsel from an objective third party to help determine your child's self-esteem and ego needs.

Remember that whatever the rationalizations are, the child must be considered. He holds the key in terms of the direction, pace, and new material you may wish to give him to change his attitudes. Ask yourself, "Is my child old enough to handle any new information?" "Is he emotionally equipped to accept this new data?" "Does he possibly need to hold on to certain ideas for a time to maintain his self-esteem?"

Questions like these will help you to focus on your child and his needs if you suspect that he is using rationalization as a defense.

Guideline #6—Use one or all three of the following criteria to determine whether or not a stepchild is rationalizing.

a. He has to search or stretch for reasons to justify his behavior.

Example: "I haven't been cleaning my room on Saturday mornings because my dad (the absent, noncustodial parent) usually calls then to see if I want to do something with him. I don't want to have to quit right in the middle of the job."

b. He is unable to recognize the inconsistencies in himself when others can see them.

Example: "So what. It doesn't matter. I'll believe what I want to believe and no one can stop me."

c. He becomes very upset or emotional when his rationalizations are exposed.

Example: "You don't have any right to say that to me. I'm entitled to my own opinion. So, shut up. I don't want to hear about it anymore. Bug off."

These are some typical responses. Remember that when people have their defenses challenged, they will usually react more with their emotions at first than with their reason.

Guideline #7—Consider sound biblical advice.

The Bible says, "Through presumption comes nothing but strife, but with those who receive counsel is wisdom" (Proverbs 13:10). "A fool does not delight in understanding, but only in revealing his own mind" (Proverbs 18:2). We know today that emotions spring from our thoughts. If you can change a person's belief system, there is almost always an automatic change in that person's emotions and behavior. Jesus long ago stated this principle when he said: "As a man thinketh, so is he." In any situation in life, be it a stepfamily or whatever, we are encouraged to change those thoughts and attitudes that do not contribute to our growth and self-fulfillment.

Questions That Need Answering

1. What are the major rationalizations my stepchild uses to explain his past hurts and frustrations?

2. Does my stepchild manifest misunderstandings of the facts surrounding his past that could lead to faulty rationalizations?
3. Does my child have a tendency to avoid expressing his feelings? How do I know that?
4. Am I aware of what my stepchildren really think about certain issues? How am I aware?
5. Is my child highly defensive and argumentative?
6. Do I have the tendency to put my child down for his opinions, or do I take the time to listen?
7. Do both my spouse and I set good examples of acceptance of our child's opinions and then gently probe and cautiously try to direct his thinking toward the truth? How?

7

"I'll Just Run Away From Everything"

What stepparent has not felt at times the sharp pain or rejection by his spouse's children? By using *isolation* a stepchild chooses to shut people out to avoid getting hurt any further.

"Sue is in the waiting room. We had to drag her down here, and now she refuses to come in and talk with you. We're so mad. She just won't cooperate in anything. We told her she couldn't watch TV for a month if she didn't come in. To get her to do anything, it seems as though we have to either bribe or severely punish her."

"Well, just try to calm down for now," we replied to these very troubled parents. "It's not necessary that she come in today. Why not leave it to us? It is probably good that we have a little talk first anyway. When our time is about up, I'll go out and get acquainted with Sue. Let's not rush this thing. Tell me a little about her—what is the reason you brought her in for counseling?"

"We thought it was necessary because she is always so quiet. But it goes deeper than that. For six years her stepfather and I have tried to do everything possible to help her to accept him. However, at the first hint of any disagreement in the home she immediately ignores him, changes the subject, looks out the window with a disinterested look, and after speaking a short sentence or two will go to her room. Discipline, cajoling, pleading with her to open up never has worked. The harder we try the more Sue seems to pull away. What can we do? We are pulling our hair out."

We replied, "A quiet response or a drawing back in stepchildren is a very common way for them to accommodate to emotional trauma. Knowing this may not make it any easier for you, but her withdrawal is working for her, or she would not constantly retreat, especially from your husband. It is, however, a costly way for her to deal with anxiety over the long haul. We'll just have to try our best to find out what's going on with Sue and help her to face her problems in a better and more realistic manner."

The next time the parents brought Sue into our clinic for counseling we worked with her to help her realize that she was making it hard for everyone in the home. Her silence was really a form of communication. She was saying, in effect, to her stepdad: "You are not really worth working out a problem with. I am discounting you as a person, and I don't value you enough to risk a confrontation or a meaningful relationship."

At first, she could not see this and even denied it, but after several sessions she began to discover that her behavior had a very negative payoff. She might end up losing a relationship that could be very fulfilling. When she saw what her avoidance was doing to herself, she decided to face the problems squarely. We're glad to report that when she began to do this consistently, the tension in the home lessened dramatically.

It is probably true that the most common ways children will try to handle difficult situations is either to repress them or to hide from them.

What Was Sue Doing?

Sue was using *isolation*—one of the more common defenses that counselors see in stepchildren. She was attempting to take the easy road of noninvolvement in her stepfamily situation. Isolation differs from repression in that the person has not forgotten the bad experience or the hurtful feelings. Withdrawing is a willful choice to back away so that the person loses the force of the painful thoughts and feelings.

A man in his late thirties told us not long ago that when he was about thirteen, his parents separated and his mother remarried. He related that he hardly ever shared himself. "I just wouldn't talk to anyone in the family unless I had to." He continued, "I was so embarrassed and upset that I couldn't bear telling other people of the breakup of our family. Withdrawing saved me a lot of pain." He admitted that his behavior helped him at the time, but the withdrawal from people affected him for years. Again, this shows that no matter how old children are when such trauma takes place, they must somehow cope with the loss while continuing with the complicated process of growing up.

This defense, while it assists a person in relieving conflict for a while, will in time put quite a strain on him. It prevents a person from being spontaneously open and free to face himself or others.

Isolation will in time usually lead to fatigue. Keeping thoughts and feelings whirling around in one's head is very demanding. Holding back takes a lot of energy. And, like repression, the use of this defense blocks feelings and in time dams up the person's ability to feel anything. This in turn prevents emotional and spiritual growth in a person. God made us social creatures—not isolated islands.

Of course, all people need some space at certain times in life. It is good to have a place where one can be alone. Jesus demonstrated this often during His three-year ministry on this earth. Frequently, He withdrew from the curious and demanding throngs. The Gospels tell us that He often went into the desert to pray, to talk with His Father, and to be alone.

But when a stepchild consistently uses withdrawal to move away from a problem, the yellow caution flags are waving. The quiet, nonverbal behavior usually signals that he may be "at war" with himself, his stepparent, or the entire family. Let us now consider some of these typical yellow flags indicating problem areas of isolation: first, some of the symptoms and then some of the causes as seen in stepchildren.

"My Kid Seems Depressed"

The first thing we want to look for is heavy depression. Some may always be expected when there are major changes in a child's life. Ordinarily, depression is short-lived and will clear up, say, in a matter of months. But it's the long-term episodes that you want to be concerned about—when your stepchild pulls away from ordinary interests, friends, and school. Generally, depression in children is not always as well marked as in adults. You see it more in their moods than in the way they behave.

Remember that the basis for nearly all depression is some form of loss, such as a friend, money, security, or self-esteem. This aids us in understanding a depressed stepchild. The stepchild was once accustomed to the biological family system as a whole unit. When that security structure is upset, it represents loss to him. Depression may indeed follow. If his confidence is shaken in one parent who leaves, for whatever reason, that too will affect his feelings of security with the new stepparent.

Withdrawal or isolation then becomes the means by which a stepchild insulates himself against having to face those conflicts with a new parent. "After all," reasons the child, "if I'm not around, I don't have to talk." It may also become a means for the child to work out his guilt. He may feel at fault for what happened to his family. If he feels that way, then depression is a way to punish himself, because depression is not only loss but hostility turned on oneself.

In most cases, the depressed child in isolation manifests many symptoms. One is poor self-esteem. You may also expect school grades to drop, withdrawal from play, petty stealing, lying, constant irritability, compulsive overeating, and difficulty in concentrating.

One twelve-year-old boy we dealt with was brought to counseling because of acute depressive moods. Billy knew what was happening, but he seemed unable to stop such moods. He even asked his father and stepmother to help, but they could not reach him. He seemed to have lost interest in everything and even talked about ending his life.

In therapy we discovered that his father denied him the privilege of seeing his real mother. "Your mother is really sick . . . she'll mess up your head." The boy held deep anger toward his father, which he could not express openly. The result? Depression.

Another sign of depression is a stepchild's refusal to eat. Watch for this. This is a symptom seen in almost all depressed people. Depression, or the feeling of melancholy, not only affects eating habits, but tends to slow down the whole body as well as psychic functions. The child may move slower as well as think more slowly.

Dr. Richard Gardner gives us an excellent, comprehensive statement on the characteristics of children of divorce who are depressed or in a state of withdrawal. There is:

> Loss of appetite; diminished interest in and concentration on studies; general apathy; loss of enjoyment from play and peer relationships; helplessness; hopelessness; irritability; obsessive self-criticisms; and withdrawal. In addition, some children exhibit feelings of impotence and vulnerability, extreme boredom, inability to complete projects and assignments, poor motivation, low frustration tolerance, and inability to use play to work out their reactions to the separation. In severe cases depressed children may become preoccupied with self-destructive fantasies, become accident-prone and unconcerned for their personal safety, and may exhibit suicidal gestures and even attempts.[1]

These symptoms of depression are sure warning flags. If your child exhibits any of them, it behooves you to find out why.

"My Child Is Either in His Room or Never Around"

Isolation is usually manifested by the child's spending an inordinate amount of time in his room. His amount of time spent outside the home will increase, or he may often be seen brooding. We asked one stepchild what he did in his room. "I just stare at the ceiling for hours, just thinking," he said. "I want to be alone."

The stepmother and father of a typical youth in conflict told us that their sixteen-year-old boy would come back home only to sleep. He'd leave extra early for school in the morning and always seemed to have a round of activities after school with friends. He somehow always managed to have money to eat out. He never talked to his parents or went with them to church or family outings. He was not rude or discourteous, just unavailable. When asked to spend more time with the family, he'd always reply: "I'm just too busy."

This story shows the problem with isolation. There never was any real opportunity for the teenager to resolve any of his conflicts with the family. He was never around.

Many stepchildren, however, use isolation to try to resolve their conflicts. They do this by isolating certain parts of their lives from other parts—home from school, church from social life, and so forth. They may act quite differently in various settings.

"My Child Seems to Cling to Us All the Time"

This is a very subtle form of isolation because it appears to be contradictory. One stepparent disclosed the fact that her stepson never, never got out of line. He always did exactly what was expected of him. He complied with any request and was far more cooperative than the normally somewhat rebellious ten-year-old. But while he looked compliant, inside he was ready for an emotional explosion. Later, it came to light that this boy had deep hurts and fear of never seeing his real mother again. He was afraid of tension and was very reluctant to talk about his real feelings.

So as not to have to deal with any trauma whatsoever, he appeared to be overly good, having everything under control, and stayed close to his parents to prevent them from judging him as a problem. If you have a child who appears to be extra "clingy," this may mean more than a need for attention. He may be trying to isolate his feelings so he doesn't have to face them. The overly compliant child is one to be watched just as much as the child who misbehaves. His overt goodness may be a cover-up.

"My Child Is Afraid to Go to School"

Another thing we've noticed while working with stepchildren who have extreme separation anxieties is that they may not want to leave the house to play outside or go to school. This is what psychologists call a "school phobia." This was mentioned earlier, in chapter three, but it also fits here in this discussion because it is a form of isolation. Because of the fear of loss, the child wants to withdraw at home.

The label "school phobia" does not fit the situation very well. Actually, the child is not essentially afraid of school. He is more afraid of parting with the parent by leaving the home. When the child's feelings of imminent loss are dealt with, the anxiety will leave. We've recommended that some parents, after consultation with school authorities, be allowed to go into the classroom to relieve the fear of separation in their child. Constantly giving in to the child's whims, though, only perpetuates the problem in most cases.

"My Child Doesn't Seem to Care"

If your stepchildren manifest a constant "I don't care" attitude, it may be a subtle form of isolation to serve as a smoke screen to keep people away. When queried, they usually do care. Youth are very aware of the overtures made to them, and they are often very grateful for those who show genuine concern. Their difficulty usually lies in being afraid to accept openly or respond because they are afraid that if they do, they will make themselves vulnerable to pain and hurt. Just knowing that stepchildren often do care can bring much relief to parents who do not understand the dynamics of the isolation defense.

Having seen some of the symptoms of isolation in stepchildren, let us now look at some of the underlying causes that create this problem for both the children and parents.

Too Much Interrogation

We have found that many children withdraw in the stepfamily because the custodial parents pump them with questions when they return from visiting the other parent. As we counsel stepchildren and establish trust with them, they often complain about getting the third degree. They worry about betraying confidences from one home to another. For example, when they visit their noncustodial parent for a weekend, they often withdraw upon returning to their regular home because they don't want to be confronted with any interrogation.

One father we know caught his son writing things down in a notebook during one of his weekend visits: "Daddy said this" and "Daddy said that." The father was furious because the boy was going back and reporting to his mother. He wrote things down in order to remember them because his mother was very demanding. The boy admitted, however, that he hated his mother's questioning. He didn't like being in the middle.

Coming on Too Strong and Too Fast

Frequently, a stepchild will use isolation as a defense when he is unprepared for the display of affection by a new stepparent such as touching, hugging, and kissing. What stepparents need to realize is that sometimes the child is either not used to showing emotions or may not want to give open affection to the stepparent, at least at first.

One prudent stepmother said in our office, "Betsy is so cold and detached—just like her own mother—but I can wait." The stepmother's attitude was commendable. However, we had to forewarn that mother that Betsy might never change to any degree. A lot would depend upon how their relationship developed in the ensuing months.

As in all relationships, time is necessary to build love and trust. When a new stepparent rushes in to form a close bond, it can overwhelm a child. Disappointment may be the result. A child will very often withdraw and become distrustful.

If the child pulls away because you've come on too strong and too fast, it may take a long time for him to begin relating to you in any depth. Be patient and it might all work out.

Terribly Embarrassed

Out of embarrassment or deep shame stepchildren will frequently try to isolate or hide the facts about their parents' separation and subsequent remarriage.

Matt, a blond-haired teenager, had a hard time in counseling telling us about his parents' situation. His face would actually flush when he talked about them.

Soon after her remarriage, Matt's mother began noticing that Matt no longer brought his school buddies around to the house. We asked him about this in counseling, and it came to light that he didn't want them to know he had a new stepdad. When asked about his real father, he'd lie by saying that he had to go on frequent trips for his business firm.

What adults fail to realize is that children aren't altogether flexible or adaptable when it comes to breaking up one home and starting another. More and more adults in today's world seem not to care about what people think about their personal lives. Divorce and remarriage have far less stigma than they did twenty-five years ago. Stepfamilies should be extra sensitive to the fact that children may be ashamed of the new situation and need help to accept it.

Conflicting Emotions

We hear a lot these days about split personalities. Watching a stepchild's behavior leads parents to think, "It sure seems as though my kid has two different sides to him." There's a lot of truth to that.

The two sides come out in the form of love-hate. Psychologists call this *ambivalence*. The normal feelings of ambivalence that a child has toward his parents in a biological family are mild compared to those in many stepchildren. Many children will try to handle their strong mixed feelings by withdrawing. The conflict can be so intense that the child will just pull away. One boy put it this way. "I could just spit nails. I love my dad so much, but I also hate him because he won't visit me." You could just see his frustration as he spoke.

Stepparents need to realize that mixed feelings are a part of the human scene. A child can both hate and love you as he can a natural parent. You may be extremely disliked because you have replaced a real parent, but at the same time your stepchild may have good feelings toward you because he appreciates your caring concern for his welfare. The following is well stated:

> Parents often ask us, "What should I say when my child tells me he (she) hates me?" Our answer is to express whatever the parent is feeling, but to qualify the answer; for example, "I don't like you either, right now." Such responses seem quite acceptable to children. They give children an outlet for their frustrations, let them know that the parents don't like them at the time, and put the situation in a time frame.[2]

Try to remember that ambivalent feelings are normal, and if a child is withdrawing, he may be doing so because he cannot handle the two emotions simultaneously. Try not to overreact. Then the sudden, blurted out statements such as "If you were my real dad . . ." will not shock nor hurt you as much. "The child is reminding him or herself of this fact as well as telling you. If you handle these situations with grace, in future years you will become the child's 'real' friend long after he or she may have given up close feelings for the original parent."[3]

Loss and Loyalty

Another major cause for isolation in a stepchild are the feelings of loss and loyalty he may have about the parent who is no longer living with him. Some children will actually choose not to get too close to such a parent if he has been hurt by that parent. Children may become aloof toward those who have abruptly changed their lives and diminished their security. They are afraid of further rejection. However, they may also have a strong loyalty toward that parent because they have a psychological need for identity with the parent.

At the same time, out of loyalty for his real parent, the child may put the stepparent at arm's length because he cannot allow himself to get too close to that stepparent. Years later, when the pressure is off, the child can stand back objectively as a grown adult and say, "Yeah, my stepdad was a pretty good fellow after all. He really did have my best interest at heart. Actually, he did more for me than my own father." But as a child, while living together, he could not allow himself to get close to his stepdad.

Adults will often say to a stepchild: "Just think, you're gaining a new parent. How great!" The child may reason, "I'm not gaining a new parent, I'm losing my real dad." When the force of that hits home, the child may very well retreat and grow sullen and unresponsive.

When children become isolated, their play activities may often center on their search for the lost parent. Their preoccupations are often with someone who has disappeared. They may also have vivid dreams in which people disappear.

Take note when your stepchild seems to be withdrawing. He could well be facing nagging loyalty feelings or rejection due to loss. Isolation is a major problem in many stepfamilies. The following practical suggestions should help you with your children.

What Parents Can Do

Guideline #1—Reach out with great understanding.

Many stepparents suffer a great deal of anxiety because the isolation defense they see in their stepchild prevents them from getting close. Isolation does not always mean noncommunication or withdrawing bodily from relationships. Take the example of a family at a baseball game. Perhaps all of a sudden a stepson might say, "Mother, do you remember when you and Daddy went to a game with me last year? We had so much fun."

That could stab the stepfather's heart, especially if he is keenly sensitive to such remarks. What a stepparent must realize is that remarks like this are a form of isolating or keeping the stepparent at a distance. This is, of course, most disconcerting and doesn't do much for warm relationships, but there are things you can do to work through it.

The first step toward getting your stepchild out of the isolation defense is understanding the origin of his behavior. In the above case it goes back to the old business of troubled loyalties. Perhaps the child wanted to reestablish loyalty to his real dad by remembering that he and his father liked watching baseball together.

In such a case, it is imporant for the stepfather not to withdraw, panic, or press. If he understands what may be behind his stepson's actions, he won't take them as a personal insult.

If you see that your stepchild is having a loyalty conflict between you and his absent, natural parent, try to help him understand that he isn't being disloyal to that parent if he welcomes or tries to get close to the new stepparent in the home.

Guideline #2—Use logic with your stepchildren but temper it with love.

Logic works better with older children—at least ten years old and above. It is particularly useful with adolescents, who are more easily helped in seeing that isolating from a problem can become detrimental in their lives. First, help them to see that if they use this pattern while they are still young, they may carry this behavior into adulthood. It may become a defense they will use to handle all threatening and confronting situations, whether it be a boss, a neighbor, friends, or a spouse. This can cause all kinds of problems, heartache, loss of jobs, and so forth.

Second, help your children realize that the longer they try to hide the pain, the longer they will prolong their ordeal. You might say something like this to your child: "No matter how much easier it may seem for you to run away from the problem, it isn't going to help anything. Let's get it out on the table and work with it. I'll help you in any way that I can."

Keep in mind that while your logic may be cogent and clear, it still may not convince your stepchild. Be patient and loving. Eventually, some of the logic may sink in.

Guideline #3—There is a time to back off.

Forcing relationships never works. If your stepchild withdraws and becomes cool toward you, try to respect his values and feelings at the moment. Be aware, however, that your spouse—the child's natural parent—may misinterpret what you are doing and become angry because you don't seem to care about your relationship with the child. Sit down and explain to your spouse what you are trying to do. Try to get his or her understanding and cooperation. And, even if your spouse opposes your plan, it is probably better to back off in some degree anyway.

You might say something like this to your stepchild: "Hey, I know it's tough. I know that you wish your real mom were here, but we have our new family now, and I'd really like to talk about this with you. Whenever you are ready to talk, let's talk." This approach may bring about a certain mellowing in the child's attitudes, more pleasantness, less defensiveness, and more willingness to help around the home.

June and William Noble offer some good advice for parents faced with a withdrawn child:

> Now, when there is a general pattern of silence with a child who lives with you or there is regular unruliness, you have to search elsewhere for clues. One of the more useful approaches is

to examine how your personality or your attitudes differ from those of the parent the child is used to living with. Are you excitable, loud, demanding, forceful? Or are you quiet, calm, soft, and yielding? If the way you are is substantially different from the way the child's natural parent is, the child's relationship with you might simply be a reaction to that difference.

"A child who has had a cool mother or a reserved father," says psychologist Frankie Mae Paulson, "and gets exposed to an overzealous stepmother or stepfather is going to recoil—sometimes in absolute fear—because they simply may not understand what it is that the stepparents want. In their fantasy they may actually see themselves overwhelmed by this." The child might grow quiet as a defense to this, or sullen and moody because it rocks her secure world.[4]

Guideline #4—Reach out with words of assurance and acceptance.

While backing off and giving the stepchild space may be the best thing to do early in the new family, you will eventually want to try to help your stepchild work through the loss he may be feeling.

Teenage stepchildren often display a flippant attitude about the separation of their parents. But their withdrawal indicates they grieve on the inside. Gently probe and get them to talk about those feelings of loss and point out the value of crying, along with the release of those feelings. When people grieve, cheering them up is not always the best approach. They need to mourn in order to work through the grief. In the child's case he will need displays of support, affection, and a listening ear.

Stepchildren will always be in special need when it comes to grief. Stepparents can be most effective if they let the stepchild know he is accepted and that they will not judge him for any feelings he might have. Getting youth to discuss these feelings is not an easy task, but with some diligence you can learn the art of eliciting open communication. "If you put forth the effort to become a friend to a confused adolescent stepchild," write Jean and Veryl Rosenbaum, "he or she will be *your* friend in adulthood."[5]

In some cases, the stepchild can be so stubbornly withdrawn that urging him to enter into conversation may seem hopeless. You may have to start with simply trying to get him involved in family activities such as picnics, rides, or get-togethers with relatives. Whatever you do, don't let the stepchild continue in his isolation defense except for reasons cited earlier. This only tells him that he can do as he pleases and makes him feel he has a certain amount of power and control as he remains an island away from the rest of the family.

Guideline #5—Encourage outside involvement.

It is critical that you guard against having your stepchild withdraw from everyone and everything. One strategy is to fill up his day with so many activities that he won't have much time to dwell on the negatives. There is an old proverb: "It's easier to act yourself into a new way of feeling than to feel yourself into a new way of acting."

As you help your stepchild set goals and plan a special day or outing, it can create a spirit of excitement and anticipation. And all the while he is planning and anticipating, he is getting his mind off his past hurts.

Stepchildren who isolate might well benefit from a reliable relationship outside the family with a good friend or a counselor in order to enhance the building of trust in adults again. Sometimes their new feelings of trust may be transferred back toward the stepparent or their real parents. This will quite naturally strengthen the unity of the stepfamily.

Guideline #6—You may just have to ride it out.

A lot depends on the child and the circumstances. Most stepchildren who are trying to isolate will work through their intense feelings of loss, grief, and separation if they are given enough space and time. Of course, if your child appears to be deeply emotionally disturbed, it is dangerous to allow them to remain withdrawn very long. In cases like this seek professional counsel.

Guideline #7—Consider sound biblical advice.

We live in a day of guided missiles but misguided men. Part of the avoidance or isolation problem today seems to be to some extent an outgrowth of twentieth century behavior. We live in a society whose values are hazy and where people try to deal with many of life's roughest situations simply through avoidance or escape. Typical avenues of withdrawal are alcohol or drug abuse. It seems that many people today believe that anything is better than trying to learn to confront their problems openly.

The Bible says, "Anxiety in the heart . . . weighs it down, but a good word makes it glad" (Proverbs 12:25). God did not make us to live in isolation. We do need one another. The apostle Paul instructed the church to "bear one another's burdens." Sharing scriptures with your stepchild, such as Colossians 3:12–17, on the value of being open and dealing with problems in a direct manner, may help.

> And so, as those who have been chosen of God, holy and beloved, put on a heart of compassion, kindness, humility, gentleness and patience; bearing with one another, and forgiving each other, whoever has a complaint against anyone; just as the Lord forgave you, so also should you. And beyond all these things put on love, which is the perfect bond of unity. And let the peace of Christ rule in your hearts, to which indeed you were called in one body; and be thankful. Let the word of Christ richly dwell within you; with all wisdom teaching and admonishing one another with psalms and hymns and spiritual songs, singing with thankfulness in your hearts to God. And whatever you do in word or deed, do all in the name of the Lord Jesus, giving thanks through Him to God the Father.

Questions That Need Answering

1. Is my stepchild withdrawing more and more from me and our family life? Why?
2. Could my stepchild possibly be depressed and I not know it?
3. Does my child show any of the following signs of withdrawal and depression:
    Poor self-esteem
    Moods of sadness
    Moping around without much ambition
    Decreased appetite
    Isolation from friends

Disinterest in school

Gloomy attitude about life

4. Have I given our stepchildren a chance to "settle in"? In what ways?
5. From what I've learned in this chapter, what are some of the best ways to keep my stepchild from isolating?
6. Is it best right now to let my child continue to isolate or to try to move in and get next to the child?
7. Do I understand from my reading in this chapter what a loyalty conflict is? Is it possible that my child might be in this bind?

8

"I'll Just Pretend Things Are Different"

One of the easiest ways for stepchildren to handle
their conflicts is to *fantasize* about them. Using the
make-believe world, they picture things the way
they would like them to be.

Steve, a twelve-year-old boy, was brought to counseling because his
school grades had dipped from A's to D's and F's in a period of one
semester. The boy was an honor student and a model child. After one
session we knew that he had a lot of anxiety because his father refused
to see him.

The boy sat in school by the hour thinking about his father—his
schoolwork no longer had any meaning. Since his father would not reveal his phone number, the boy had only the past to think about. His
mind constantly wandered to the good times when they used to fish together or worked in the garage on a woodworking project. He longed
for those special times with his dad at Dodger Stadium watching baseball games.

Counseling helped Edwin, the stepfather, to realize he needed to get
next to the child by talking. It was not long before things began to turn
around. Their many talks pulled the boy through and, as expected, his
grades went up.

What Was This Boy's Problem?

Young Steve was engaging in what is called in psychological terms *fantasy formation*. He had a problem concentrating on everyday life. This led him to daydreaming and helped him somehow to rub out the deep hurt he was feeling. Thinking as he did about the past made him forget such nagging questions as: "Where is my father?" "Why doesn't he come around anymore?" "Doesn't he love me?"

As a defense, fantasy is created or stimulated by frustration and wishing for a better life. Such mental images grow out of strong needs that must be met in one way or another. Fantasy helps the person to fulfill those needs by picturing things as he would like them to be. In fantasy the emotional desires are catered to.

We can see this illustrated well in Steve. Through fantasy he could imagine being with his dad at ball games or fishing. Many wishes cannot come to pass, but the fantasies reduce the hurt and conflict because the person pretends that those desires do take place. Steve was simply trying to reduce his feelings of rejection.

The problem with fantasy formation is that it usually deludes the person into ignoring the fact that his wishes may never come to be. And, like many of the other defenses, fantasy prevents the acceptance of reality, and its overuse can cause reality to become fuzzy in the mind. Because young Steve fantasized so much, he had a very hard time accepting his relationship with his stepfather as it was.

In younger stepchildren fantasies are shaped by their own limited capacity to grasp confusing events. The absence of suitable explanations about their world often leaves them bewildered. This will cause them to rely on their own immature explanations.

Children who already have felt the sting of the separation of their parents believe they are deprived of life's essentials. They may even fantasize about not having enough food or toys.

As we found in Steve, daydreaming is a natural outgrowth of the fantasy defense. Daydreaming's only value is that this kind of fantasizing may temporarily relieve stress. You can see why this would be a popular defense with most stepchildren. But it becomes destructive when it substitutes imagined and easier accomplishments of the "make-believe" for the real world, where hard work is often necessary to deal with life.

The fantasy defense is much like denial except that the person who uses denial tries to remove totally the facts about the past. In fantasy, the individual gives consideration to the facts but tries to change them through wishful thinking.

We have noticed that the fantasies in stepchildren seem to center on the "lost" parent for the most part. Over the years, as we have counseled children and adults, we see that the less direct contact people have with a certain person the greater the likelihood that they will develop fanciful distortions about that person. Stepchildren frequently develop distorted fantasies because they have no way to test them against reality, when it comes to the absent parent. Such thoughts will usually take two forms: (1) idealizing the parent as almost superhuman or (2) devaluing them—acting as though they didn't exist. When a child devalues the absent parent, it is usually because he is angry and has feelings of being abandoned by that parent.

Children are known to visualize almost anything. This is certainly no less true for a stepchild. As we counsel stepfamilies we recognize five basic fantasies, although there are many others. These fantasies help stepchildren in particular to somehow restore self-confidence and to relieve the feelings of personal loss. Remember, these fantasies are held without much awareness of the connection between the real-life event and the wish. Let us now look at each one, realizing that stepfamilies are fertile soil for their germination and growth.

"I Want to Keep My Absent Parent Good"

We discussed this at great length when we looked at the denial defense, but it crops up again in fantasy. One key defense in people who see themselves as failures or find themselves in negative circumstances is to fantasize, "I am a conquering hero." The stepchild who gets caught up in this kind of wish usually identifies with the noncustodial parent who takes on the hero qualities.

If a child has fantasized this way, he may become quite defensive if something critical is said about the noncustodial parent. During a counseling session one boy told his stepfather, "You're talking about my dad and you have no right to say that." The boy's stepfather happened to know the facts, but the boy had fantasized them away. In addition, the boy had not been allowed to see his natural father very often. This perpetuated the problem.

Self-blame often enters into this fantasy when the child makes out his absent natural parent to be a "conquering hero." This self-blame is very subtle. The child may not at all blame the stepparent, but in essence he puts the blame for his parents' separation upon himself. In that way he doesn't have to deny his absent parent's infallibility. This protects his need to keep this parent omnipotent or perfect. The self-blame fantasy makes the child feel more secure as he fantasizes his natural parents to be people who are good, right, just, and fair.

Then you may have the situation where pressure comes from the other direction, outside the home. Leslie Westoff hits the nail right on the head when writing about the idealization of the absent parent. He tells about one father who told his boy: "Call me if you are unhappy. You can always come and live with me."

Of course, the father had no intention of taking his boy in, but the boy did not know this. To him, his dad was generous, really sensitive to his needs, and a very loving person who would give him anything. But unfortunately, this boy had totally forgotten what his dad was really like. Therefore, he built up an image of a generous parent that was pure fantasy. As long as an absent parent encourages such a thing, the child will not cooperate with the parents in the stepfamily.[1]

In normal child development it is important for a child to idealize his parents as being bigger and smarter than he is. This gives him a healthy identity as an aid to self-esteem. Such fantasies, however, must be realistic and as close to the facts as possible. The stepchild who refuses to acknowledge the real facts surrounding his absent parent will usually be reluctant to accept the new stepparent who enters his life.

"I Want to Believe That I've Had a Terrible Time"

This second type of fantasy is what we call the "suffering hero" syndrome. Here the person imagines that he is really suffering. He has some great handicap, is sick, abused, or misunderstood. In the fantasy the person imagines that when people are made aware of his plight, they feel very sorry for the way they have treated him. Then he gets attention that he needs or thinks he deserves.

Gracie was one such stepchild who believed that both her real parents and stepmother were very cruel to her and never tried to understand her hurts. This nine-year-old admitted that she spent countless hours imagining that these adults were very sympathetic and caring. She said that these thoughts helped her to get through the day. When we talked with her in counseling, however, she began to recognize that the fantasy wasn't paying off. She could see that she was filled with self-pity and people were upset with her because her fantasies were causing her to be cold and distant at home. Even though cold and distant, she could see that she believed that these same people owed her everything because of the divorce.

When we helped Gracie to give up such notions, it was amazing to see the changes, not only in her attitudes, but in the way people in her home began reaching out to her in a more accepting way.

"I Want to Go Back to the 'Good ol' Days' "

There's a little of this fantasy in all of us. Stepchildren are no exception. Their fantasies can often run wild. It's amazing what you can do with your mind. In fantasy you can actually change the past into anything you want.

Stepchildren often have the tendency to read back into time and events what really wasn't there. They think about the "good ol' days" but fail to realize they weren't really so good when they were going through them. Many children in stepfamilies don't want to face this, so they will simply change the past by imagining that things were better than they really were.

We once read about a woman who vividly used this fantasy while growing up as a stepdaughter. The tragedy was that it destroyed a good relationship with her stepmother. The woman, whom we'll call Betty, related that she fantasized about her natural mother not out of ignorance of the facts but because she had a need to rewrite history. Betty's mother had been a drug addict, forcing Betty to flee from home when she was an adolescent. In the following years she would have nothing to do with her mother even though she became debilitated. When she died, the daughter showed no outward signs of grief.

There was a sudden turnabout when Betty prepared for her own marriage. Her fiance's mother became very ill, and his family spent every available moment caring for her. It was more than Betty could bear, remembering how she had "rejected" her own sick mother.

Betty's father remarried a short time after her mother passed away. A few months passed. Betty, who had been open, happy, and loving toward her stepmother, became very cold and distant. Things worsened as time went on. She began putting pictures of her mother up on the wall, and she complained that she really had a miserable time while living with her stepmother. Betty told the same story to her fiance's family.

What she had done was to create a myth because her mother had died. She chose to forget the ugly past of her drugged mother, and she wrecked the relationship with her stepmother. Betty had a great need to change the past because she couldn't handle the way she acted before her mother died. Turning against her stepmother was a way of redeeming herself for the way she behaved when she was younger.[2]

Again, this story shows that a child never gives up on the natural parent and is prone to forget the negative past by fantasizing that it wasn't so bad after all.

"I Want to Keep My Parent Alive"

In some stepfamilies, the problem is not an absent, living parent but a parent who has died. Children can become very adept at creating fantasies about that dead parent. Keeping that person alive in the mind can work very well for a while. But as time goes on this may become more serious because the child is unable to test his ideas in real life.

Many stepparents who have married a widower or widow know what coping with this fantasy is like. Some are not allowed a parental role at all, due to the fact that they cannot ever measure up to the stepchild's conception of the dead parent. Without ever communicating it, a child can fantasize to the degree that he builds the parent into something beyond the realm of comparison. And, over the years, whenever a problem comes along, the child will blame the stepparent, because the dead parent—who was close to perfection—could certainly never have been at fault.[3]

Living in the shadow of someone else can be most disheartening, especially when you get the idea that that person could do no wrong.

One stepfather named Larry complained that his stepchildren very much wanted a father before he married their mother. They gave him a lot of love and encouraged him to decide to marry their mother.

"Before I married their mother, the children and I had so much fun together. They enjoyed sitting on my lap. But as soon as I moved into their home, the kids turned on me. It almost took my breath away. All they'd talk about was their dad, who had died in a plane crash two years before. They idealized him so much there was absolutely no way that I could even come close in measuring up to him."

Such stories disclose the strong and binding fantasies stepchildren can develop for a parent who has passed away. When these ideas become cast in concrete, the building of a good child-stepparent relationship is almost impossible without tremendous understanding on the part of the adult.

"I Want Dad and Mother Back Together Again"

We have already seen in previous chapters the powerful need most stepchildren have to see their natural parents reunited. Remember, that when divorce occurs, most children are convinced that they were somehow responsible for the breakup of the marriage. Once they believe this, they often develop a fantasy structure that leads them also to believe that they are powerful enough to reunite their parents. It is common for stepchildren to work openly to achieve this goal, even long after their father and mother have remarried and a stepparent has joined the family.

Twelve-year-old Lisa illustrates how stepchildren will sometimes maneuver or manipulate to get and keep the parents together even after they have remarried. On one occasion, after her father came to pick her up for a weekend visitation, she feigned getting hurt. Her father and mother had been talking in the living room. She "fell" in the bathroom and made it look as though she were really hurt. Both parents rushed to her aid. Lisa's performance kept the parents together for at least several minutes. At other times Lisa would stall for long periods of time while her parents had friendly conversations. She either could not find things to pack, or she'd take an extraordinary amount of time washing her hair.

Indeed, many stepchildren will go to almost any length to perpetuate their fantasies about their parents getting back together. They may interpret any little friendly gesture as a sign of reconciliation. For some, this desire has lasted for many years, and some children tell us they want their folks together even when they know it would not be best for the family.

We see this fantasy manifested in small children given the Thematic Apperception Test (TAT). In this kind of test they are asked to respond to picture cards and tell a story about what the cards are saying to them. Many of the stories told by stepchildren describe persons as their natural parents. The children often conclude their stories with the words "and they lived together happily ever after" or something close to that.

The purpose of this fantasy is (1) to restore the family in order to block off the acute pain of the separation and (2) to relieve guilt if they believe they contributed to their parent's breakup. Imagining that the parents are back together relieves the child's guilt.

Fantasies in children do run wild. If you believe your child is using them as a defense that is preventing adjustment in your stepfamily, you should consider the following guidelines.

What Parents Can Do

Guideline #1—Allow your children to fantasize freely.

Most fantasies will disappear when a child grows older and adjusts to life. Just knowing this may bring some relief to a frustrated parent or stepparent. In the meantime, remember that the child who creates a "make-believe" situation does so to deal with loss. His dreams are one way he tries to cope with his anxieties and thwarted hopes. For the first few months, anyway, allow the fantasies and be extremely careful about even mildly criticizing your stepchild for such "hoped for" wishes as his desire to relate to his absent parent or wanting both natural parents back together again.

One of the best ways to help Johnny, who has a great need to fantasize, say, about a father who pays virtually no attention to him, is to allow him to talk about his father freely and as often as he wishes. You might add, "Your father did love you, Johnny, in his own way, and such memories are good to have."

Some might ask, "If I encourage the child to dwell on past happy memories, won't this cause him to daydream all the more?" The answer is a decided no if you give him lots of love and emotional warmth. As he is accepted and given the freedom to express his fantasies, the child will feel much safer with you and be able to live more in the present, rather than the past. The mere acceptance of the feelings behind your child's fantasies will help him to relax and deal with his problems. As you gain the child's confidence, he will talk more freely about his pain, as well as his expectations and broken dreams.

Discussing a subject once is usually not enough. You will have to go over it again and again. Recurring feedback is vital to help the fantasizing stepchild work through the problem. Again, you will need to be candid but kind, honest but sensitive, to the child's feelings.

Guideline #2—Try to ignore grandiose or exaggerated statements.

As you seek to make it safe for your child to fantasize, don't let "off the wall" comments get to you. Some of these might be:

"So what if Dad did this or that—there's nothing wrong with him."

"Any place has got to be better than this house."

"Nobody around here ever tries to understand me."

"Yeah, everything that goes wrong around here is my fault."

Ignoring such statements is one of the best ways to allow the free expression of your child's fantasies. It is not wise to *constantly* confront or put the child down for them. If the fantasies are challenged too strongly at first, it may rob the child of a coping mechanism for dealing with the feelings of rejection or abandonment.

When your stepchild does talk about ideas that are absolutely ridiculous to you, it is usually best not to comment other than to say, "My, that's interesting," "How did you come up with that?" or "Tell me more about it." Again, don't overreact!

Guideline #3—You also want to be firm.

While you want to create a warm and accepting atmosphere for your stepchild, there are times when you will have to confront certain fantasizing because it isn't helping the child. One of the clearest examples of this is when the child continually fantasizes that his natural parents might get back together. As we've already pointed out, most children won't give up on this possibility. Be firm but very kind and final as you conduct open and frank discussions about the problem.

Clearly explain to the stepchild that the natural parents are not going to reunite. Another strategy is to talk about the divorce openly. This will also help to discount any fantasizing about the reuniting of the natural parents. As the children begin to hear the facts, it will help them to realize how impossible it is for their natural parents to reunite. A divorce is a terrible thing, but what is done is done, and the new family must go on. The children must hear this over and over. They must realize that the new family has been firmly established and is not going to go away because they wish it could be so.

Guideline #4—In some cases allow the child to go live with the absent parent.

The best antidote for fantasy is reality. We often suggest to parents that a child should live for a period of time with the absent parent if the child tends to overfantasize about that parent. We do not condone constantly threatening to send a child to the other parent. This is a form of manipulation, and it is wrong to use this issue as a means of leverage.

The counsel offered in this guideline refers to a circumstance where the child is *constantly* fantasizing about an absent parent's being totally good. In this case, you might say to the child, "Go over there and live if you think it would be so great!" Such a move for the child will have a wonderful way of removing the "halo" around the absent parent.

Living with a parent, even for the shortest period of time, helps to disclose his humanness. For the child who has the tendency to distort, close contact with the distant parent will change those fantasies in a hurry because the child has a better chance to see him as he really is. This minimizes any possible illusions the child may develop about the absent parent.

Guideline #5—Seek cooperation in disciplining from the child's absent parent.

Day-to-day parents have to say no! They have to say, "Billy, it's bedtime." "Mary, you have to turn off the TV now and get to your homework." A parent who lives away and is not that involved in a child's life seldom has to discipline. Because a child naturally dislikes discipline to begin with, he will fantasize that the distant parent wouldn't "be so mean."

When the stepchild goes to the house of the absent parent, it's usually for a good time. This only keeps alive the fantasy that the parent is only "good" and never unpleasant. Then, too, the absentee parent often will try to make up for lost time by overindulging the children when they do arrive for their weekend visit. Their time together may be taken up exclusively with fun and games. This "Disneyland" relationship can really get things out of perspective for the child. When he is back home, he may have a tendency to think of the other parent as better because "we always have a great time."

If your stepchild is possibly caught up in this fantasy, we would strongly encourage you to talk to the overindulgent parent. Ask that person to ease up on his "merry-go-round" approach and to apply discipline when the children are in his hands.

You will probably have to talk very gently about the subject because noncustodial parents are often very defensive people when it comes to interpersonal relationships with their children. This parent may not cooperate with you. Because of defensiveness and hostility, this parent may take this request and twist it by telling the child, "Your mother doesn't want me to have any fun with you any more." This kind of distortion can sabotage what you're trying to do.

If your ex-spouse is unable to discuss issues rationally or is too stubborn to cooperate, then you have a problem. Try to help him see that cooperation is in the best interest of the child, and this attitude may change. Remember, try to concentrate on the child's needs—not yours!

Guideline #6—Teach your stepchild that he can love more than two parental figures.

Parents and stepchildren both need to realize that there is room in the human heart to love and accept another parental figure, such as a stepparent.

Stepchildren also need to be helped to recognize that if they accept a stepparent, it does not mean that they are in any way rejecting or giving up a real parent. A professional counselor can be of much assistance in helping your child break down fantasies such as we've discussed and therefore be more open and accepting of a stepparent.

The question is often asked of us: When does a stepchild need counseling? Counseling should at least be considered in the following situations:

1. *Home.* When a child manifests a repeated behavioral problem or when there is deep depression
2. *Social.* When a child retreats from his peers and no longer seeks friends
3. *School.* When a child departs from routine or normal behavior in the classroom or when there is a consistent falling down in schoolwork
4. *Emotions.* When a child manifests repeated unreasonable emotional responses

We always recommend bringing the whole family in when counseling is deemed necessary. It is important to look at the whole family structure in order to get at the root of the problems.

Guideline #7—Allow a stepchild to recall and talk about parents who have died.

Stepchildren need to be allowed to talk about any natural parents who have died. If a stepchild senses your disapproval when he talks about the deceased parent, he will develop a deep sense of fear or resentment. If this happens, it will make it much more difficult for the child to accept the new parent.

Guideline #8—*Help your stepchild realize that fantasies don't change things.*

One of the best ways to help break fantasy patterns in stepchildren is to get across to them that in and of themselves, thoughts don't make anything happen. In working with stepchildren who have fantasy problems, we will often tell them a fanciful and absurd story about how a boy's or girl's thoughts made such and such happen. They begin to giggle and see how ludicrous the story is. You may want to try this approach to help the stepchild see that thoughts alone have absolutely no control over a person's behavior or events.

In breaking down fantasies that prevent growth, intimacy, and the acceptance of reality, bear in mind that stepchildren can gain control over their lives to a large extent by just learning to separate factual event and circumstances from impossible fantasies.

Guideline #9—*Provide a lot of security on special days.*

We've noticed that holidays or festive occasions like birthdays can be a very difficult time for a child in a stepfamily. He may strongly fantasize during these times. He will frequently become moody or sullen because of his need for both parents to be there. Wise are the parents in the stepfamily who will recognize the child's needs during these periods. Reaching out to them by making these occasions very special and personal will go a long way toward getting them through.

Guideline #10—*Consider sound biblical advice.*

Fantasy and dreams make a very real contribution to our lives. For example, fantasizing is the starting point for every invention. But the fantasies we have discussed in this chapter can produce the opposite effect if they are all-consuming.

There are examples in the Bible of several people for whom fantasies worked to their disadvantage. Old Jonah became consumed with his fears and fantasies over the city of Nineveh. He didn't want God to forgive the city and give it the same spiritual status as his own people back in his homeland. He sat alone outside the city under the shade thinking about all that had transpired. The experience proved fruitless and nonproductive. Because of his fears, he wanted to die. This shows what can happen. Negative thoughts and fear can lead a person to want to drop out on life. Getting your children to face reality will overcome their nonproductive fantasies.

Sometimes your child's fantasies may get you extremely upset. The Bible clearly indicates that real love involves acceptance. Consider the following pieces of advice:

"Love is patient, love is kind, and is not jealous . . . love . . . is not provoked . . . bears all things . . . hopes all things, endures all things" (1 Corinthians 13:4–7).

Real love, according to this text, means that you will not bear grudges against a child who has the need to reject reality.

Questions That Need Answering

1. Do I think my child is fantasizing to his detriment? If so, what is he doing that makes me think this?
2. Have my stepchild's teachers at school reported that he daydreams a lot in class?
3. Does my child have the tendency to overaggrandize my ex-spouse, without seeing his or her faults?
4. Does my stepchild tend to indulge in self-pity to get attention?
5. Am I aware that to some extent fantasizing can aid my child to cope with anxiety related to our stepfamily?
6. Do I allow my child to express his fantasies openly?
7. Do I put my child down when he does open up?

IV

The Stepchild Who Attempts to Fight Back

Most parents in the stepfamily have experienced anger in their children—when they lash back in one way or another. This is called *fight*. In these three chapters you will read about three typical defenses stepchildren may use to deal with their anger. They are *displacement, projection,* and *regression*. These terms are not difficult to understand. They all have to do with such basic questions asked in many stepfamily homes as:

1. Why does my child seem to be so hostile all the time?
2. Why does my child seem to read into situations things that are not really there?
3. Why does my child go back to acting like a much younger child or a baby?

9

"I'll Take It Out on You Instead"

Stepchildren often lash out with angry words and
actions. Many of them use *displacement*. They are
discharging pent-up feelings onto safer objects. In
many cases the child takes it out on others.

Mrs. Harris, an attractive mother of three, smoothed her skirt and
fidgeted about in her chair for a few moments. She was visibly upset.
After a short silence I broke in. "You are upset aren't you? Why don't
you tell me about it?"

"All right, I've tried for a couple of days to decide whether I should
see someone like you. Maybe it's rather silly, but something has happened that has really thrown me. I'm really mad and frustrated right
now. So much so that I've been crying ever since I received this letter."
At this point, Mrs. Harris began sobbing.

After another period of silence, I responded. "What I'm seeing is
that you are hurting more than you're angry. Could that be true?"

"Well, yes, I think so. It's like this. The letter I'm holding came from
my husband, Bob's, daughter. She is fourteen. Her name is Susan and
she lives about 200 miles away, so we seldom see her. Bob is unable to
take advantage of his visitation rights because of the distance. So we
decided to have her go with us on a three-week vacation if her mother
agreed.

"I never got to know my stepdaughter very well and had the highest
hopes of accomplishing this while we traveled in our motor home
around the West. I can't tell you, Dr. Juroe, how hard I tried to make it

comfortable and pleasant for Susan. I really tried to make her fit into our family and to help her get along with my children. I cooked the best meals I possibly could and even offered to make some of her favorite dishes. All in all we got along without much friction. Bob and I had just a couple of spats, and the children had some minor squabbles, but for most of the time, I thought, we were one big happy group.

"Now, we got this rotten letter. In it Susan stated so many nice things about her dad and thanked him all over the place for such a great time. She did not have one nice thing to say about me and said that I was moody and quite nasty most of the time. That is just not true. She even alluded to the fact that she might not want to do this again if I went along.

"Doctor, I just can't believe it. I did everything in my power to make it nice for her. What could have possibly gone wrong?"

We began to discuss what might really be going on with her stepdaughter and how she, as the stepmother, must not take it so personally.

What Prompted Susan's Actions?

This opening story shows us vividly how some stepchildren deal with their anger. Susan was redirecting her hostility onto Mrs. Harris, when she was really upset over her mother, who had left her father several years before. Susan's behavior and resulting letter is what psychologists call *displacement*.

Displacement is the shifting of feelings from a more frightening object to a more neutral or safer one. This defense also can be used to disguise self-contempt by unconsciously turning the contempt upon other people. This can make a person snobbish or revengeful. Because the individual doesn't want to recognize his own feelings, he may dump contempt onto others rather than toward himself.

Displacement may take many forms, and there are numerous illustrations to show how it works. For example, a child who has been spanked or thwarted by his mother may kick his little sister or break up his toys. A man who comes home from work all bent out of shape because his boss chewed him out may begin to yell at his wife for some minor thing or kick the dog. He's displaced his anger because he is afraid to express it at his boss for fear of losing his job. Instead, he vents it on his wife and dog. These objects, for the moment, are less threatening to him, so it is safer to use them.

Susan's anger was misdirected. She was dumping on Mrs. Harris. This caused disharmony in the extended family. That's the price to be paid when these defenses get overused or misused. Other emotions can be displaced as well, but anger is the one predominantly seen in stepchildren. In most cases it is much more healthful and less painful in the long run to face and work out those hostilities than to avoid them through displacement. Susan needed to deal with her natural mother. That way she would better see her stepmom for the person she really is—someone who is trying to be a friend and to love her.

Incidently, when Mrs. Harris came to understand that her stepdaughter was not really angry with her, she became much more relaxed. She wrote Susan a letter, and she forgave her. We're glad to report that the last we heard, Susan has followed the advice of her father to confront her real mother about her feelings of hostility over the divorce. Mrs. Harris also reports that Susan is nicer to her now that she has been able to talk to her real mother about these things.

Children living right in the home blow off steam by doing things that are often irritating, hurtful, and insulting as a way of expressing what they are feeling. Their *acting out* behavior can be anything from using crayons all over a wall to speaking rudely or obscenely to teachers at school or fighting on the playground. Others rebel, perform acts of violence, get into drinking and sex. Nearly all of this is acting out of anger.

Children who wind up as juvenile delinquents are always angry about something, and the anger is usually traceable to their parents. In fact, it is probably more accurate to say that juvenile delinquency should be called parental delinquency in many cases. Whatever they do, acting out is destructive. Stepchildren with this problem really need help. Let's look at some of the typical problems that can arise in the stepfamily where the children are using the displacement defense.

Stepparent—You May Be the Target

As stepchildren act out their anger, they will often pick the stepfather or the stepmother as the target. We've noticed in counseling with stepfamilies that the displacement defense is frequently directed at the stepparent of the same sex. For example, if a boy is upset at his real father, it is likely that the stepfather will get the repercussions.

Boys, by the way, have a tremendous need to identify with their natural fathers. With another man in the home there is confusion for a boy if the stepfather is unlike his real father. While boys sometimes get angry at stepfathers, we have seen in prior chapters that the real target for displaced feelings is often the poor stepmother. One of the earliest writers on stepfamilies says:

> Anger at the very person of a stepmother takes all kinds of forms; in a study of troubled stepdaughters, one accuses her stepmother of having an affair, another says her stepmother makes her do all the housework but pays no attention to her; a third claims her stepmother is jealous of her.[1]

When children display hostility like this, a stepparent is often placed in a precarious position. The parent often believes the best thing to do is to crack down with stiffer and harsher punishment, and so the vicious circle begins. The child rebels more and more and the parent then cracks down even more. Before long you have an open conflict.

Helen Thomson describes this vicious circle very aptly when she says that at this point the stepmother often just gives up. When obedience is not forthcoming, she feels hurt and bitter. Her husband doesn't understand. She feels in competition with the children's mother and less capable. She then hesitates to discuss her troubles. She knows she is hated, and after a while she doesn't even care what relatives think. She just wants the kids to mind her. When things don't work out she will grow resentful toward the children's father, who doesn't help enough, and long for the children eventually to leave.[2]

In nearly all cases the stepparent is the target for a child's unconscious displacement of anger. And, it does not matter how good that parent may be. Remember the anger underneath is at the real parents who caused the original pain by breaking up the home.

Brothers and Sisters, Too

Feelings in a stepchild may also get misdirected onto the stepbrothers or sisters. A child may just refuse to interact or cooperate with the other children. Tremendous rivalries are most typical. There is manipulation for attention and, sometimes, acts of personal insult or injury.

We well remember a fourteen-year-old girl who was given the responsibility of caring for her little stepbrother and stepsister after school. Both her parents worked. Jill despised her stepmother. For several months, until the truth was exposed, Jill threw the small youngsters around and badly mistreated them. She made her brother and sister lie if she hurt them.

Many stepfamilies are in trouble because of the refusal of one or several of the children to adjust to their new brothers and sisters. Because of their agitated feelings, they are unable to handle the complex aspects of the new family. Tension and fighting result from the rivalries and jealousies.

When stepchildren get angry at their stepbrothers and sisters, it may not be displacement, but it is always a good idea to try to find out. If your stepchild is constantly bickering or angry, it could possibly be displacement of some kind because he's really upset at you and your mate. Try to get to the bottom of it because it should be a matter of deep concern.

Rebellion Against Authority Figures

Sometimes stepchildren will provoke punishment by their parents through certain acts of defiance or misdeeds revolving around the house rules. This may be because of the child's need to lessen the feelings of abandonment. He may even be willing to endure pain in order to have the reassurance that the parents will still be there even when he misbehaves. The rationale might be, "I'll find out if my stepparent really cares about me. I'll rebel and see what he will do."

We remember one very angry stepchild who had just entered his teen years. He blinked his eyes furiously and bit his lips and fingernails incessantly while in counseling. It took several sessions before he would look us in the eye. Angrily, he would often reply to questions with this rejoinder: "What do you want to know that for?" His answers were typically one word or less. He was defiant to say the least.

Ron came only a few times after the parents were informed that therapy was useless because he did not want counseling. "It's just a waste of time," we said. Later on we heard from his school counselor that this lad had been expelled from school. It was very clear from his behavior that Ron was displacing his anger onto us, his teachers, parents, and classmates. He surely couldn't be angry at all of them. He did say in one counseling session that he hated his stepfather. That was a clue right there, perhaps. Then he added, "I'm going to give hell to anyone who gets in my way."

If your stepchild displays anger toward adults who represent some kind of authority to him, he may very well be angry at some person in the stepfamily. You don't have to be a trained counselor to spot this. If you're perceptive, you might be able to get your child to face squarely the real conflict he is unable to deal with.

Runaways

Running away from home or ditching school are common forms of displacement behavior. We've counseled many stepfamilies who have had to track down runaways. The stepchild may not only be acting out displaced hostility, but he might be trying to find reassurance that he is not going to be abandoned and that someone cares. The child also places himself in the control position. He may fantasize himself the rejector rather than the rejectee.

This thought helps the stepchild to cope better. "If someone is going to be separated, then I will decide when and how it will take place." It is much like the jilted lover who lets everybody know that he broke it off first. This saves him the humiliation and protects his self-esteem.

Running away from home or ditching school are direct signals that parents need to recognize. The stepchild who acts out this way is trying to tell his world something. Punishment isn't always the answer either. Trying to get next to him is.

Stealing

A female probation officer once asked us to find out why a certain seventeen-year-old high school dropout had become a compulsive shoplifter. When he arrived for counseling, against his will, it did not take long to uncover what was behind it all. The boy admitted that his broken home had thrown him for a real loop and that he no longer cared. He even flippantly remarked, "And, I don't care if I have to serve time in the clink!"

Stealing by stepchildren is usually a symptom or sign that the child is struggling with the feelings of emotional deprivation. The best way to handle this problem in most cases is to help him to dispel the feelings that precipitated the acting-out behavior. The child must, of course, be told that it is wrong to steal, no matter what the age.

But severe punishment should be tempered because it may heighten the very feelings that caused the trouble in the first place. Too harsh a punishment could confirm in a child's mind that his fears about himself are correct: "See, I am a nobody. I am no good. I deserve the worst."

Remember, when a stepchild steals, he is doing much more than seeking personal gain. Greed may be a part of it, but such behavior may point to the displacement of some feelings that have not been faced by your child.

Sexual Promiscuity

Sexual acting out is a very tragic, far-reaching, and severe form of displacement. Like most professional counselors, we have found that immoral behavior can be a real problem in stepfamilies.

We are mainly referring to sexual activity outside the home by stepchildren. Let's not forget that one main reason for this is the absence of role models to help children grow emotionally in their psychosexual development. For example, an adolescent girl might become sexually promiscuous when her own father leaves in a marital breakup. She finds herself relating to a stepfather who is not serving as a good male model or giving her a good example of moral integrity. One serious problem is incest. Stepfathers, for example, sometimes force themselves upon a stepdaughter in a sexual manner and then frighten her into being quiet about it. That's what's happening far more often than most people want to admit. They cringe at the very thought—it sounds so perverted—but it is reality in many stepfamilies today.

One fifteen-year-old stepdaughter was known by all the boys at school as "easy." When we talked to her about her behavior, she frankly admitted that she was trying to fill an emptiness that she felt because her family was broken up. This girl's story is a typical example of the enormous power of the sex drive during the teen years. Her normal family security had been destroyed, and she became angry about it and displaced that anger by using sex as a weapon.

The absence of a natural parent's authority and values in a home appears to spark sexual activity because the development of the child's conscience may be inhibited or lessened. The reason the conscience doesn't develop properly is that there is no longer that strong bond between the child and the parent of the opposite sex. Now the child often is dealing with an opposite-sex stepparent. In the new environment the child may not have the opportunity to test his sexual feelings in proper ways. Cuddling, hugging, and touching the opposite-sex parent is a forerunner for sexual maturity because it is within limited boundaries.

For example, a female can sit upon her daddy's lap and enjoy the warmth, hugging, and closeness of their relationship without fear of sexual involvement, which helps her test her feelings. In this way she learns about maleness, trust, and respect, which is the foundation for a healthy and mature sexual relationship with her husband-to-be.

But when a stepparent moves in, this kind of relationship is usually very hard for the girl to develop. The child feels strange around the stepparent. The child may not want to cuddle or be touched. If there is this lack of touch, such deprivation may cause the stepchild to act out her sexual impulses in search of the hoped-for love that is absent because the parent has left.

Abusing Animals

If you notice that your stepchild is hurting his pets or other animals, it may be a clue that the child is displacing some kind of anger. We have also seen that with many stepchildren animals take on a new significance. Some children will become more caring and loving toward them because they come to realize that animals—especially dogs and cats—can nearly always be trusted.

Yet, we've seen some stepchildren become extremely cruel with animals. One teenage boy used his .22 rifle to shoot at animals in his neighborhood. He was also very cruel to his own pets. When finally caught and questioned in counseling, he admitted to being angry at his natural parents, who both had remarried.

The above are just some of the more typical problems that we've found in stepchildren who are displacing their anger in one way or another. Let us now look at some specific guidelines you can use if this is a problem in your home.

What Parents Can Do

Guideline #1—Deal adequately with your own hostility.

You need to lead by example in expressing your own anger in a proper way. When conflict that triggers anger arises in your own life, let your stepchild see that you are not displacing it but dealing with it appropriately. Be a good model. If you don't know how, then read some good books that show you how to deal with anger. Take an assertiveness training course. Get into therapy if you have real difficulty in this area.

Guideline #2—Help your stepchild learn to face his anger, if possible, when he first feels it.

It is vital in the stepfamily to get your child talking about his anger. Teach the child to say, "I'm angry about . . ." or "I'm mad because . . ." Through practice the child will learn the invaluable lesson of feeling more comfortable about having anger, will learn to be more direct, and get the feel for actually using words that convey his real feelings.

It is not easy to get the flow started again after the original impulse has left—but it is not impossible. A good starter is to get the child to relate the particular incident that triggered the emotion. Then say, "Tell me about it." It is best not to make any judgments or interpretations at this time. Do not say, "You shouldn't feel that way," or "How could you take it that way?" The youngster will not get it out of his system or see the whole situation in perspective if he feels condemned in any way. Only if he speaks out will he get relief. As a child is accepted for his feelings, he won't feel abandoned or prejudged. But if the parent or stepparent shows disinterest, it will only increase his frustration and resentment and will encourage him to save up his anger or displace it in wrong ways.

Always help your child to realize that "stack blowers" are the very persons who don't know how to express anger. Help him to see that allowing hostility to build and build and suddenly explode is a poor way to live. Always encourage your child to be honest with you about his anger. But at the same time you will have to teach him the proper way to express it.

Guideline #3—Teach stepchildren appropriate ways to drain off hostility.

One of the best ways for a child to work off steam is by channeling it into sports or recreational activity. This is especially helpful with smaller children because they have a tendency to express their feelings more in actions and less in words.

We have often recommended that parents whose children have problems over anger get their youngsters into the YMCA, Boys Clubs, Little League baseball, youth activities at church, or even painting or music. Ballet for girls is another excellent medium to discharge the intense energy welling up inside. Hitting baseballs or punching bags helps to work off aggressive hostility.

This kind of displacement is helpful. It is what the psychologist calls *sublimation.* It helps a disturbed youngster gain mastery over his hostility. It is far better for him to take out his anger on a ball or a bat than on his stepfamily.

Guideline #4—Deal with destructive anger firmly and fairly.

Stepchildren can be masters at playing the rules of one home against the rules in the other. They will often say the stepparent is grossly unfair: "You're too strict. My dad is not that way."

Both parents in this situation need to confront the problem directly. The natural parent needs to reinforce the authority of the stepparent and let his child know, "We have our rules here regardless of what rules they may have in the home with your other parent. You must obey them as long as you are with us." The child has to be made to see that the new family structure, of which he is a part since he lives there, is the primary unit.

The stepparent might say to a child who does not accept his authority: "Look, this is the way I do it. I cannot take the place of your father, but I'm responsible for you as long as you live here. Therefore, you are going to live by my rules."

Always confront the hostility and acting-out behavior firmly and gently. Take bed-wetting. You should be aware that it may be due to repression, as discussed in chapter three, or some physiological problem. But it can also be an unconscious, unwitting act of hostility. As a stepparent, you might confront the situation this way: "Look, I know you're angry and don't want me in your house, but you can just come right out and say it—you don't have to wet the bed. I'm not moving out because you want me to, but I understand how you feel. I might feel the same in your position."

Discipline is vital because all children need and want limits. But consistency is needed from you and your mate. Most psychologists agree that acting-out behavior may actually be a way a youngster is asking for prescribed limits. It's a way your stepchild may be testing you as parents, so pick up on it.

You must deal with the problem of discipline very early in the relationship. The child must know right away that values and rules will be established and that there will be a measure of expectancy that they be followed. Stepparent, especially, do not become a doormat. If the children sense that you feel no right in correcting their bad behavior, manners, or habits, they will gleefully continue in many cases to be obnoxious.

Unless roles are clearly identified, some stepparents are going to feel timid about punishing their stepchild. And, some natural parents may resent any interference by the stepparent. If you're going to share another person's life and children, then the two of you must present a united front. Openness will help to guard against a divided front. In many instances we have suggested to parents that they openly discuss limits and contracts in front of their children. If it is done in a family get-together, then the children cannot manipulate you by arguing: "Mom says I don't have to do what you say."

The following issues ought to be addressed—most of them even before the decision is made to remarry.

1. What types of discipline has the natural parent used in the past?
2. What are the stepparent's expectations concerning discipline in the home?
3. How much of a role is expected by the natural parent or the stepparent?
4. How much of a role is the stepparent willing to play in disciplining the stepchildren?
5. What part is the natural parent willing to allow the stepparent in discipline?
6. Are they willing to back up each other 100 percent?

It is also important that both must be in relative agreement on what is and is not desirable behavior. When roles and boundaries are set forth at the outset, there is no need for any continued testing by the children. They come to know exactly what to expect.

*Guideline #5—**Don't lecture.***

If you have a child in your stepfamily who is continually acting out with hostile behavior, constant lecturing will do little good. When you are doing all the lecturing, the child is left with nothing to say. The messages you are sending out get short-circuited in his brain, and he will tune you out. We find in counseling stepparents who have junior high and high school stepchildren that it is helpful to tell them that by the time a child is eleven or twelve, he has incorporated all the adult ideas and values he's going to get. Some reiteration along the way won't hurt, but all parents should remember that the teenager has heard it all before, and it does little good to turn on the "record" again for the 120th time.

Our approach to parents who find themselves continually lecturing or nagging their children in the stepfamily is as follows. It is not so important that the child do the dishes just the way you want or make the bed-sheet folds a certain way when he makes the bed. It's not the rules that really count—it's whether you are building a relationship where there is open and honest communication. Don't let the rules come ahead of the relationship.

Guideline #6—Help your children to see the uselessness of displaced anger.

If you have a stepchild who is continually angry and in trouble, help him to see that picking fights in school and other kinds of hostile behavior never really gain anything. He may be able to blow off steam for a short time, but the same old anger will pop up again and again. What you must talk about with your child is the cause for the anger. Help him to get at the bottom of it. Teach him that as he takes out his anger on others, it only costs him in self-hatred and the loss of his friends.

Guideline #7—Beware of peer influence.

The stepchild acting on his own will seldom behave as violently or openly as one who is egged on by others. Parents might do well to discover any negative influences and prevent the child from running with that crowd. Be careful here because too much involvement on your part may actually drive your child toward the negative peer group. Find ways to discourage your child from being with other youths who make him angry. Remember, you always have the right to keep this kind of negative influence from entering your home. Show your strong disapproval. Then, all you can do is hope that your child gets the message.

Guideline #8—Fads can be your ally.

Believe it or not, fads can serve a good purpose when you have angry stepchildren. Fads are especially important because they give adolescents and teenagers a sense of identity. Remember that many fads serve as an outlet for hostility and rebellion. A child often is using a fad as a way of releasing hostility against adult authority. Choosing clothing or hairstyles that may be particularly odious to parents may well serve such purposes. Parents who constantly criticize or harp on the subject may be falling right into a trap. The child is probably feeling a lot of satisfaction out of "getting to" the parents.

In most cases, fads are really harmless outlets, and one of the worst things you can do is try to force a youngster to give one up. Try to appreciate that fads are among the most innocent and innocuous ways for youth to let go of hostility. No matter how much the fad may irritate you, consider the alternative: drug addiction, teenage pregnancy, or criminal behavior. Fads can actually be looked upon as blessings.[3]

Guideline #9—Show your child genuine concern for his needs.

You will give your child less reason to be angry if you show him that you really care. Real concern for him, his interests, his needs, his feelings will all help to cut down on his provocative acts to gain attention. When he does lash out with anger, you need to reach out to him to find out what his needs are. Find out what's "bugging" him. Tell him, "You've got my attention, so what's really gnawing at you?" Find out if there is some unfulfilled need that has surfaced in an unacceptable way.

We've found that consistent affection can go a long way. Many needs can be met by genuine love and caring. A stepchild who may feel unloved will often reason: "What's the use of being good? I'm not appreciated anyway for who I am or what I do around here. No one cares and neither do I."

Heaps of praise, lots of hugs, back rubs or foot rubs when your kid comes home tired, after a basketball game, for example, can go a long way to help reach a child. Work on positive reinforcements.

Guideline #10—Don't overreact when dumped on.

If your stepchild really dumps on you, you can save yourself untold misery and frustration if you can remember that he may not really be angry at you. Be careful not to take this behavior too personally. Unfortunately, the stepparent who gets the vented anger often reacts the same way in retaliation.

However, if you realize that the child may be displacing anger, you can better curb your own emotions. Realize, too, that your child is probably trying to cope by shifting his real emotions to a false target (you). This may help you to relax. The key is not to be too quick to overreact.

Guideline #11—Consider sound biblical advice.

Perhaps the best passage in the Bible on anger is found in Ephesians 4:26. "Be angry, and yet do not sin; do not let the sun go down on your anger." When your stepchild has undealt-with anger inside, he is letting the sun go down on his wrath as he plays his displacement games. Don't play these games with him but try to understand what he is doing, accept what you can, and deal with it in a positive way.

The apostle Paul, in the same passage, goes on to state that stored-up anger that is not dealt with properly gets misdirected and exaggerated. Such hostility can lead to hate, malice, and bitterness. Displaced anger does break relationships. If your child can see this, it may alter his behavior.

Also, King Solomon offers us this advice: "A gentle answer turns away wrath, but a harsh word stirs up anger" (Proverbs 15:1). This is a much-needed principle for those in stepfamilies who may have the tendency to overreact. Deal kindly and graciously and you may become pleasantly surprised at how much less your children will displace their anger.

Questions That Need Answering

1. Am I aware that my stepchild may have hidden anger? How?
2. Does my child act in inappropriate ways? What are they?
3. Do I really understand what displaced anger is, and can I see it in my child?
4. Do we make an effort in our family to help our children deal with their anger? How?
5. Am I a bad example to my stepchild by displacing my own hostility?
6. Can I be mature enough not to take my stepchild's anger so personally if I suspect that it is displaced onto me?
7. Are we making our stepchildren accountable for their inappropriate ways of acting out? In what ways?

10

"I'll Make You Out to Be the Bad Guy"

Many stepchildren place blame for all their troubles upon others to enhance their self-esteem and to get control of their lives. The use of *projection* masks a child's true feelings by attributing them to someone else.

Tom was a fifteen-year-old stepchild whose father had remarried when he was about twelve. Tom refused to talk at any length with his stepmother. About the only responses she could get from him were "Good-bye" in the morning when he went to school, "Please pass the potatoes" at meals, or "Good night" before retiring at night.

Desperately, his stepmother tried to get him to talk. She'd frequently ask: "What's wrong, Tom?" "Oh, nothing," was his usual reply.

Tom's real mother, who lived in the next county, was a woman of ill repute. She had numerous affairs and many people knew about it. While Tom's father was married to her, he tried everything to help her change her ways, including spiritual counseling with their pastor and in-depth psychotherapy. Nothing was effective. Tom's stepmother, on the other hand, was a highly moral and warm woman who liked to have close relationships within a family.

In counseling, Tom's father and stepmother attempted to find some answers. "Why is it so difficult for him to communicate at home?"

This problem had led to great tension and frustration. After a number of visits the therapist compiled much background information about Tom to help him realize what he was doing.

At one appointed session, the therapist glanced out his office window before they were to begin. He saw Tom trudging very slowly up the long stairs toward the office. Watching him dawdle up to the second floor, a thought flitted through his mind, *My, how difficult the past sessions have been. Tom's body language tells me a great deal. He really doesn't want to be here. His defenses have been so high. However, I hope this session will be a real breakthrough.*

He walked to the door and greeted the lad. "Hi, Tom, how's it going?

"Ugh," was the reply.

"You don't seem very excited to be here."

"Oh, sure, I want to be here," Tom replied.

After a few more introductory exchanges, the therapist began to press the point. "Tom, in our past sessions you told me that you didn't want to go live with your mother. You said, too, that you liked your stepmother and appreciated her very much. However, she does not feel you mean this or want a relationship with her. You seem also to be hiding your true feelings."

"Why should I have a relationship with her—she's just a dumb female? After all, she's just another woman, and I don't trust any of them. Even the girls at school are dingy, and I like to give them a bad time."

"Don't you date?" said the counselor.

"Aw, sometimes, but I'd much rather go with the guys. Girls just want to get serious too fast, they get too hysterical, and they're seductive. They're very selfish and really don't care about me. They use me and all my friends—from borrowing money to getting us to take them around in our cars."

Let's Examine Tom's Responses

Tom was engaging in what psychologists call *projection*. He was finding fault with his stepmother, all the girls in his high school, and all women in general. He was associating his stepmother with his own mother and her immoral conduct. It came to light that Tom really didn't trust any women. He had almost no interest in the opposite sex, and he scorned girls in every possible way. Sometimes he was downright mean to them in school.

Tom did reveal that he had sexual feelings, but deep down he greatly feared that he might become immoral just like his mother. With his counselor's help he gained insight into his real problem. He was projecting his feelings for his real mother onto his stepmother. This prevented him from getting close to his father's new wife.

Stepchildren like to use projection because it works. For Tom the use of this defense became a very convenient way of putting distance between himself and his stepmother. This defense is much like displacement because it shifts the target for the expression of feelings. When projection is overused, it can easily cause a person to become paranoid.

Put simply, projection is perceiving thoughts and feelings and action in someone else to avoid seeing them in yourself. This avoids or conceals anxiety and was what Tom was doing in relation to his mother and stepmother. This little game becomes a convenient way for not having to deal with certain people. In Tom's case he was refusing to accept his stepmother because he put her in the same category as his own mother. The attitude was conscious. What was unconscious was the transference onto other women of his own feelings about his mother.

Placing blame reminds us of Flip Wilson, who got laughs for years on his weekly TV show with the line "The devil made me do it." This throws blame elsewhere. Projection takes numerous and varied forms. For example, students say, "Everyone else cheats on exams, why shouldn't I?" Or, the politician projects onto the media his own fears, weaknesses, and feelings of inadequacy by accusing them of irresponsible reporting.

Projection conceals several emotions, but with a stepchild it appears mostly to be fear. The following are some of the major projections we've encountered while working with stepchildren.

"I Can't Trust You"

Remember that projection is a mask. The stepchild who projects mistrust onto others is really covering up the mistrust he has for himself because he feels guilty. For instance, a child may believe erroneously that he had some part in the breakup of his parents. If the child feels somewhat responsible, he will search for another person to dump on in order to get rid of guilt. When he finds that person, he feels greatly relieved for the moment.

This particular kind of projection can be seen in the following story. Curt was a teenager who constantly argued with his stepmother, Evelyn. His sneaky behavior caused suspicion to reign in their relationship. Everything came to a head one weekend as the hurling of threats hit its mark, and Evelyn screamed back to her stepson, "I am not putting up any more with your accusations when you yourself are the one who is rummaging through my things. I have no privacy! You have no right to snoop through my mail! Furthermore, I do not read your mail or go into your room to search for anything. How dare you accuse me of your own deeds?" With that remark, Evelyn left for her sister's house to cool off and reevaluate the situation. She sought her pastor's help, who in turn suggested that she come to us for counseling.

With help Evelyn learned about the true nature of the interplay with her stepson and why it was happening. Eventually, Curt came in too. This was a very tough counseling situation. It could have ended in disaster if they had not been painfully honest with each other. Curt admitted that he believed he caused much of the trouble between his real parents. They frequently fought over him in such matters as discipline and choice of friends and activities. We helped him to see that this was not the basis for the divorce of his parents. Once he understood this he was released from his guilt. His self-esteem was enhanced and he gained new trust in himself. This spilled over into his relationship with his stepmother. He stopped checking up on her, and he made a pact with her to " 'fess up" to his feelings so they could talk more. Evelyn was a real trooper, and when she could see that there was a way out of the tunnel of trouble, she knew she could endure. Curt also came to appreciate the efforts they both made.

We've found that mistrust is the most frequent projection used by stepchildren. It is an easy way out for them because by engaging in it, they attempt to find fault in others for their own frustrations and conflicts.

"If You Weren't in the Picture, Everything Would Be Great"

We have said many times in this book that the stepparent's presence is usually a prolific breeding ground for unresolved emotions in the stepchild. Many children, as we have noted, may not want the stepparent in the picture. Instead of facing those bad thoughts, the child will distort by projecting the idea that the stepparent doesn't want him in the picture.

Sandra was just such a child. She constantly complained to her mother that her stepfather didn't want her to be very involved in their lives. For example, the family often spent its weekends going camping. Sandra frequently and firmly stated: "I know that Jerry doesn't want me around—I can just tell." The mother and stepfather were not the rugged outdoor type but felt they needed to expose their adolescent daughter to more family recreational activities. In essence they were camping more for her enjoyment than their own.

When Sandra revealed her feelings in the matter, her family, which included an older brother, was stunned. Her brother replied, "How could you feel that way about Jerry—he's always inviting you to go. I don't feel that way, why should you?"

This is a classic example of how projection works. When we project on others, they become mirrors, reflecting our true feelings and thoughts instead of theirs.

"I Can't See the Good in You"

This projection in stepchildren blinds them to the good in others. This attitude is not often verbalized, but it may come out in such statements as "I can't see what my dad sees in my new stepmom." Again, this projection is probably a glimpse of how the child feels about himself: "I can't see what others see in me." He wouldn't say that, but he believes it.

We have also seen stepchildren who project their bad feelings about their parents onto the stepparent. In either case, a child who is projecting sees his stepparent as having the same bad traits he's seen either in himself or his parent. This is particularly true for the stepparent who is of the same sex as the natural parent.

Examples are plentiful. When curly-haired Rachel counseled with us, she said her mother was always putting her down. At the same time Rachel felt her stepmother was too critical. Calvin, a chunky adolescent boy, complained about his father who seldom ever saw or phoned him. He believed that his stepfather was not interested in him either. Projections like these really run rampant when a child has a poor self-image. They definitely prevent a deepening of relationships because they serve to keep the person who is the target of this defensive tactic at a distance.

"You Really Don't Want to Accept Me"

This is a very common projective technique used by stepchildren to prevent closeness to someone in a stepfamily. The child can't face the fact that he could possibly reject that person. He sidesteps the issue—in his mind—by making the other person reject him first. This nicely takes care of any possible guilt. "I didn't reject her first—she did me." The child feels less guilt that way.

We once worked with a ten-year-old girl named Donna Jean. She was very bright—almost too much so, because she was a master at conniving. She was asked by the parents of her stepfather to visit in their home for two days during her Christmas vacation from school. She did not want to go but would not dare say no. She was too frightened to say anything because she feared they would reject her. As we talked about it in counseling, she reasoned: "I don't want to go because they don't like me." We knew that her attitude was very wrong, because we talked to the stepgrandparents. They adored her. When we probed further, it came to light that Donna Jean really didn't like them. It was difficult for her to admit this, so it was easier to place the feeling of dislike upon them: "They don't like me."

These are some of the major projections that children in stepfamilies use. Like other defenses, stepchildren use these devices to elevate their self-esteem, which has been damaged through such feelings as fear, guilt, and hurt. They also serve in some way to provide the child with the desire to gain some kind of superiority in the new family. "After all," he reasons, "what I do or think to hurt them in no way compares to what they've done and thought to hurt me." If successful, this line of false thinking may help to bring momentary relief from any negative feelings.

Stepparents also project. Because of their own happiness over the remarriage, they project their gladness onto the kids. This is where the "all one happy family" syndrome comes from. The parent does this so he won't have to face his own fear of rejection or failure. Ironically, while the parents are projecting their happiness onto the child, the stepchild will often project sadness onto the parents because that is the way he feels.

For example, the stepchild may burst into the house and exclaim: "Boy, this place is like a tomb." The parents look at one another with puzzled glances. They can't understand this statement because they feel happy. He continues: "Everyone around here is so sad." This may really throw the parents into a tizzy because they don't feel this way at all.

Interestingly, the plot thickens. The child who projects this way can, without realizing it, try to sabotage the remarriage, making the parents sad—the very emotion he projected upon them in the first place! When projections go on like this between parents and stepchildren, both become blind to the situation and each other's way of looking at things.

Let us now look at some of the ways parents can better manage this very deceptive defense in their children.

What Parents Can Do

Guideline #1—Evaluate carefully to determine if your child is projecting.

Just how does a parent know if his child or stepchild is projecting? There are several key clues to look for in the child. Here is a partial list to help you evaluate or assess the situation.

Is your child disclosing irrational thoughts about someone in your stepfamily? Is he being illogical about someone? For instance, a child may say to his natural, custodial parent, "My stepdad doesn't always show me that he cares," when in reality the stepparent cares very much and has demonstrated it in many ways. Often, to perpetuate a projection, the stepchild ignores what the stepparent is doing.

Is your child distorting the facts about a circumstance or a person he is having a problem with in the stepfamily? If the child is actually distorting truth, you may be sure your child is projecting for some reason. Remember, there may be some truth to what he is saying about a person, but if the facts are twisted, that will be your clue. For example, a child may say, "My stepmother cannot be a good person, because she stole my dad away from Mom." Such a generalized notion is probably a projection that needs to be dealt with.

Is your child reading into the meaning of events things that are not really there? Listen when your stepchild makes a statement like this: "This or that happened because . . ." They may often twist meanings by misunderstanding the causes behind events.

Is your child manifesting any of the following characteristics: guarded, secretive, touchy, supersensitive, devious and scheming, or questioning of the loyalty of others? These features may be indicators that your child is indeed projecting.

Does your child make exaggerated claims; does he sometimes make "mountains out of molehills"? Is he critical of others but unable to accept criticism of himself? Is he stubborn and highly defensive? Is she always looking for hidden motives and special meanings in other people? Does she avoid intimacy with people in the stepfamily or extended family except for those in whom she has absolute trust?

Guideline #2—Work on getting your stepchild to trust you.

In stepfamilies, mistrust is the basis for most projections. Children are prone to project mistrust because of past hurts. Therefore, it is vital to try to break down such mistrust if you can. But remember, it is not easy. You can cope with this by realizing that mistrust is perfectly normal. You should expect it to some extent because the child has no way of testing the trustworthiness of his new stepfamily except by being suspicious at first. After all, adults in the child's first family dramatically let him down. Why should he now trust a newcomer in a new situation? Don't be surprised if you are met with a great deal of resistance because of this.

Be patient and realize that building trust is like building love. It takes time. You will have to offer affection and understanding time and time again in order to get your stepchild to open his or her heart to you. The replacing of shattered trust will be very slow going. Don't take it personally.

Consistent caring, keeping your word, and fulfilling your responsibilities to a child are the best ways to break down mistrust.

Guideline #3—Deal directly with your child's projections.

As you deal with the child, you make him face up to his distorted thinking. You've got to do it quietly, gently, and patiently in a nonthreatening manner. Otherwise, there will be all kinds of fireworks because he will be defensive. You will probably have to go slowly. Just let him know that he is not thinking straight. You can say something like this: "Hey, Bill, what you're saying just is not true. Now, here is what really happened." Or, "Bill, you have twisted the situation. That isn't true. You know it is not true, and I know it is not true, so please get it straight." If he bristles, back off. You don't always have to approach the child in a very serious tone either. You can confront by teasing or in a fun manner. This helps to break tension.

Also, help the child see how he is distorting, and when he sees this, ask him to change. Try to show him how unreasonable or foolish his projections really are. Get your stepchild to face squarely his own responsibilities, weaknesses, and difficulties. Getting a child to admit to error can be very effective in eliminating this defense.

Teaching your child to say, "I'm sorry," or, "I was wrong," is another way to help him give up this unhealthy defense. Help him to realize that blaming others may make him feel better or more safe for the moment, but it won't work later on because of the wasted opportunities to have meaningful relationships.

Guideline #4—If the child continues to project, take him into counseling.

Because the projective defense is often difficult to spot, you might want to consider the services of a trained counselor for your child.

Remember that projection is a very insidious defense. Most step-children are unaware of what they are doing, and it usually takes someone else to point it out to them. In many cases only a psychother-apist may be in a position to do this.

Guideline #5—Consider sound biblical advice.

The Bible speaks of projection when it mentions the man who finds fault with others but can't see any problem with himself. "There are those who curse their father and mother, and feel themselves faultless despite their many sins" (Proverbs 30:11,12 TLB). There are many other proverbs in the Bible that are addressed to people who are right in their own eyes, while looking down their noses at others. The worst thing you can do is to lecture your child, using such strong verses to condemn him. These verses simply give you some information on the destructive character of projecting on others and elevating your-self. Remember, too, that it is not so much what you say, but how, or the spirit in which you do it. Be as noncondemning as you can. At the same time, however, don't be too soft or naive. Do your best to let your child know the self-defeating payoffs when projection is used.

You might approach it this way. "Hey, Johnny, there is a little story in the Bible where Jesus said, 'And why do you look at the speck . . . in your brother's eye, but do not notice the log that is in your own eye?' (Matthew 7:3). Jesus was talking about people who were unfairly judging other people. They were pointing out faults in others when they had bigger faults themselves. Now you are doing the same thing by putting all the fault on so and so. It is not right. You need to look at yourself more and see what you might be doing to make our home an unhappy place, and then do something about it to change the atmo-sphere around here."

The Bible would encourage you to help a stepchild to focus on his specific needs and responsibilities in the relationships within the fam-ily and take his eyes off others. Instead of projecting, he needs to allow trust to develop and, especially, to give his new stepparent a chance. If he does not, he is denying the family the privilege of strengthening all ties.

Principles to Remember About Projection

1. In stepchildren, *projection* has more to do with feelings of guilt and fear, while *displacement* has more to do with anger.
2. The way a stepchild feels or thinks about himself is what is projected on another person.
3. A child is more apt to project on a stepparent because it is safer than projecting on a natural parent.
4. Mistrust is the main thing that a stepchild projects on others.
5. While an attitude about a person is consciously known, the child is unaware of his projection.
6. Direct confrontation is a way the child in a stepfamily most effectively gets rid of his projections.
7. A stepchild who is projecting often acts paranoid: "Everyone dislikes me."
8. A stepchild uses the projection defense because he has already been hurt in one emotional situation and now is afraid of starting a new one.
9. Projection is a form of displacement but differs from it because it is a more passive way a child fights back against his hurts.

11

"I'd Rather Go Back to Being a Baby"

When a stepchild longs for attention or fears abandonment, he will often want to go back to a time when he was feeling more secure. *Regression* often stumps the parents, but they need to realize this is one way the child refuses to go on with his present hurts.

"Jackie," her father said, "from now on when you come to our house, I don't want you to call your new mother by her first name. I want you to call her either Mom or Mother."

Jackie's real mother brought her to counseling because she noticed her ten-year-old was acting more and more like a small child. Her father lived in the next town with his new bride. Forcing his daughter into a relationship with his wife began to have some serious effects.

Her mother reported that Jackie's behavior was highly regressive. She'd pout over the smallest thing if she couldn't have her way. She'd stomp her feet when she became angry. She also became very clingy both at home and at school. Her mother couldn't sit next to her without Jackie's wanting to sit on her lap. Her fourth grade teacher noticed a sudden change, too. Jackie came to school early to help and would linger in the classroom following school after all the other kids left. She'd often interrupt conversations other pupils were having with the teacher.

When this pretty little blonde ten-year-old came into counseling, she brought along her coloring books. Her mother reported that coloring was something she had not done for a couple of years. This type of behavior seemed to become more acute right after her father brought her home from his visitation weekend. And, when her dad came to pick her up every other Friday evening, she would seldom be ready. She'd stall by constantly going into the bathroom to check on her hair and clothes. Her small suitcase seldom was packed to go.

Jackie told us in counseling that her father frequently lectured her about his new wife. "You just have to love her. You have to accept her. She's now a part of our family." But she could not bring herself to call her stepmother anything but Irene. Deep down she admitted to hating this woman because she believed she caused the breakup of her father and mother.

Unquestionably adding to the hurt was her father's attitude. When she did not attempt to get close to Irene, he'd become gruff. Also, he was often gone most of the time on those weekends—either working or going fishing or bowling with the boys.

Why Did Jackie Behave This Way?

It is quite clear that Jackie was feeling loss. Her father, trying to force her into a relationship, didn't help either. The conflict in Jackie produced a great need for attention. She sought this attention through childlike behavior. When any child does go back to earlier behavior patterns, you may rest assured that something is bothering that child. She is saying somehow, "I'll just fight it all by going back to some sort of babyhood." This is what Jackie was going through. She obviously didn't want Irene around. Her way to handle the trauma was to use the defense of regression.

Regression is the defense whereby a person chooses (often unconsciously) to retreat to an earlier time in life when it was safer, more comfortable, and happier. It is an escape from anxiety. We classify regression with displacement and projection because it is a form of fighting back. The major difference is that the first two are more aggressive tactics, while regression is more passive.

Put another way, a stepchild will react like many grownups. Whenever a person meets frustration, there is a tendency to long for happier days. We all do this to a certain extent. Who hasn't wanted to be "babied" at times, especially when they're sick? These desires are regressive longings for days gone by when there was less tension, more pleasantness, deeper satisfaction, and perhaps more security.

The important questions to consider are: (1) How long does one stay regressed and (2) To what extent does one stay there? Let us now look at some of the typical areas where one might expect regression in stepchildren.

Smaller Children Are More Susceptible

If your stepchild appears to go back to infantile patterns, you may be sure he is regressing for some important reason. This defense is usually found in smaller children. Bed-wetting, temper tantrums, and a child's fantasy play are just a few ways younger children disclose possible regression. In fantasy play you might see a child become preoccupied with such behavior as feeding, protecting, and cuddling animals or dolls.

Regressive behavior may show itself in many different ways. Thumb-sucking may be common. Baby talk is also frequent with younger children. A more demanding attitude, too, may denote a deeper childlike regressive tendency. The child may also feign stomachaches and headaches. Temper tantrums may be expected when a child uses this defense to get attention.

One stepmother complained that within a few short weeks after her marriage to Katie's father, the child began whining about everything. She wanted to be pampered and demanded that her father always put her to bed. Even if he was very late coming home, she would wait up for this ritual. She refused to go to sleep until he came into her room to tuck her in and say good night. This isn't quite the behavior you'd expect from a nine-year-old.

It is at the ages of four to seven that young children more commonly regress by sucking their thumbs and wetting or soiling their clothes. One five-year-old stepchild in a family we worked with carried a blanket around in the house just as she used to when she was two years old. She greatly missed her daddy and seemed to be extremely jealous of the attention her mother gave to her new husband.

In young children there can be a dire need to have a person in full view at all times. The child who is regressing is trying to hold back or mark time in order to gain some strength for the future. Such behavior can be quite exasperating for the parents because household routines are often disrupted. The increased need to care for such children will often add stress for the parents.

Regressive behavior in younger children is an effective defense against the panic and threats encountered in the new stepfamily. If prolonged, it may mean a deep emotional disturbance is developing in the child.

Regression Is Seen in Adolescents, Too

Regression is an almost certain defense in youth of all ages when some great trauma hits them, like the loss of an original family. The use of this defense seems to be heightened when a stepparent comes into the picture. For many children this replacement of the lost parent creates a situation of regression to the helplessness of the infant state.

Drew, a thirteen-year-old boy, came into counseling because he began wetting the bed. His father had left his mother for another woman about six months before. The father made few attempts to contact the boy or anyone else in the family; he just seemed to drop out of existence.

But now, his deep disappointment over his father's lack of concern and response to him were so intense that Drew became more childlike. What was the force that pushed him backward? It was a nagging fear that his father would be totally unavailable in the future years and that his new stepfather would never be the companion his father once was. His fears and anxiety seemed to be the root cause of his bed-wetting— something he had not done since he was about four. When Drew finally realized that his father would not make himself available for whatever reason, he began to turn toward his stepfather with a more open attitude. The bed-wetting then diminished remarkably.

An emotionally healthy girl in a biological family at times can become jealous over her mother's relationship to her father. This is normal, and she usually can learn to handle it. If circumstances change, this same girl in a stepfamily may draw heavily on the defense of regression by clinging and clamoring for attention from the father only. At the same time she may push her stepmother away. This draws attention to herself and thus provides reassurance of her father's love once more.

One fourteen-year-old girl constantly bothered her father when he read the paper or watched TV. She'd hang onto his shoulders or insist on getting onto his lap, as well as make all kinds of unreasonable demands on his time. It was not uncommon for her to want to be taken some place as soon as he got home from work. She'd whine until he gave in. This way she could have him all to herself. This behavior is what you'd expect from a younger child. Her mother said, "Thelma acts just as she did when she was about six or seven." This girl was strongly competing with her stepmother.

In an adolescent regression can also be identified by his becoming a loner, shutting out the relationships he has with school friends.

It is well to remember that the trauma of divorce can easily drive a child into regression. He will be so discouraged and hurt that he will not want to progress in his development in life. Many children feel so helpless that they don't want to move on. Therefore you might expect, especially at first, that there will be temporary regression. This unhappiness is a reason for providing comfort for the child, but you do not have to be overly alarmed at first.[1]

If unhappiness is prolonged, depression and regressions are quite another matter and need to be watched carefully lest your young person develop an underlying pathology whereby he will just refuse to adjust and grow. This could lead to severe social maladjustment later on.

A new stepparent arriving on the scene is not the only cause for regressive tendencies in stepchildren. There may be other reasons. We'd like to cite two.

New Arrivals Can Be Upsetting

As adults at times may be threatened by new people coming into their lives, so is it true with children. When parts of two families are blended, there will be power plays to obtain attention.

We have discovered firsthand that one of the best ways to bond a stepfamily is for the new parents to have a child of their own. A new baby can be a great blessing and be a constructive force in a stepfamily. In our home it brought the immediate family closer together. Sometimes, however, a new baby can bring a lot more anguish to an already stressful family. A new brother or sister may cause the stepchild to regress to earlier behaviors long since put aside.

When Moral Values Are Lost

We have seen that some stepchildren use regressive behavior when their parents carry on sexual relationships outside of marriage. It seems to be a way for them to fight back. Numerous adolescents we've counseled have actually expressed feelings of being betrayed by such a parent. The fact that we live in a very sexually loose society does not seem to make a stepchild more tolerant of this behavior in his parents. It really does bother most children and makes them extremely uncomfortable.

Immoral conduct by parents can decidedly throw off ego development in children. Without a moral parent in the home helping to instill proper values and a conscience, such youth often become overwhelmed with the anxiety of it all. You can expect that when this happens, stepchildren may begin not only to act out, run, or go into an acute depression but also to regress by being more demanding and childlike.

What do I do when my child goes back to younger behavior? Here are some practical suggestions.

What Parents Can Do

Guideline #1—Provide positive reinforcement.

When a child's regression is in its acute stages, it can drive a child's parents to exhaustion. A clinging, overdemanding stepchild is a child who is regressed. It is not a situation, however, which cannot be overcome—with some patience.

Remember that such a child is probably threatened by insecurity and, especially, a separation anxiety. Many situations may arise, about which a parent knows nothing, that may stir up this old anxiety in a child. As we have often seen, a child who has suffered the loss of a parent often fears he will be abandoned again. Both the natural and step-parent must combat this with positive reinforcement by doing everything they can to make the child feel secure. As the child feels more secure, he will have less reason to regress.

Guideline #2—*Don't always give in.*

Because regression is such a typical coping mechanism, it is often used by stepchildren and can be tolerated for a brief time. Don't let the child be allowed a free hand too long, however, because regressive behavior may get a strong foothold. Then the defense will be far more difficult to break.

For example, a child should not be allowed to stay home from school unless there is a definite illness. Consider that it might be far better to risk sending a supposedly sick child to school than to allow a behavior pattern to develop that could eventually evolve into some kind of psychological disorder.

When a child refuses to eat, there usually is no real problem. If the stepchild persists in being fed after he has learned to eat by himself, the parent should not bow to this whim. Eventually, the need for food will take over, and usually the child will out of necessity feed himself.

Guideline #3—*Consoling a regressed child may be necessary.*

Your child should not be allowed to regress too long, but at first, rather than being scolded for childishness, he may need a lot of sympathy. When one original parent is not there, the child will probably feel hopeless and desolate. Both the stepparent and natural parent may need to provide nurture.

Guideline #4—*Be careful not to overindulge your stepchild.*

If a child refuses to follow through on his responsibilities while behaving like a smaller child, disciplinary action of some kind is warranted. Overindulgence by a parent who is always catering to a child's every whim may contribute to regressive behavior. Overindulgence may fill for some parents a neurotic need, but in the long run it only slows down the process of adjustment for the stepchild.

Guideline #5—*Try to understand the self-defeating quality of regression.*

For a stepchild, retreating to earlier developmental levels is an easy way out. He doesn't have to be as mature. He doesn't have to grow and change. In the long run, though, the use of this defense by your stepchild will be less satisfying. If you see this defense at work in your child, you will want to try to find out what is going on in his mind and work on encouraging him to change.

Guideline #6—*Help your stepchild to refrain from competing with you if you're a stepparent.*

A good way to assist your stepchild to stop being a baby is to arrange for the child to have special times alone with each natural parent. The stepparent, for example, might want to push a stepdaughter toward her father by encouraging her to see him. You or your spouse might want to call the father. "Jeannie is regressing here. She's acting as though she's only three. Why don't you take her out to lunch so she can get some needed attention from you. Can you help?" Such a call would serve the purpose of helping the girl learn to accept attention and affection from her father in an appropriate, more grown-up manner, as differentiated from little-girl ways of sitting on his lap.

The child could also be encouraged to visit friends or relatives. This helps a child grow up. The experience of getting packed and leaving helps him to get interested in things outside himself.[2] If you encourage your stepchild have private time with each absent parent, you will be less apt to be placed in competition with that parent.

Guideline #7—*Consider sound biblical advice.*

"Hope deferred makes the heart sick; but when dreams come true at last, there is life and joy" (Proverbs 13:12 TLB).

As both the natural and stepparent seek to make a child's dreams come true by making him feel secure, they will do a great deal to combat regressive behavior. The child then will find it less and less necessary to act like a two-year-old, but will naturally move on in his emotional development.

Questions That Need Answering

1. Have I noticed that any of our children appear to be acting like younger children? How do I know that?
2. What is the possible reason for this regressive behavior?
3. How long has my stepchild been regressed?
4. Do I pamper my child if he is seeking attention? In what ways?
5. Do others see regressive actions in my child?
6. Am I reinforcing regression by giving in too much to my child? Why do I do that?
7. Am I aware that if a child is regressed for a long period of time, it may mean that he may be a deeply hurt child and it may be necessary for professional help to bring healing?

Conclusion

We have tried to give you an overall view of some of the more common problems encountered in most stepfamilies. We hope we have not given too pessimistic a view. We have not said that a successful stepfamily is impossible—it is simply different and more difficult to achieve.

With better tools now in your hands you should be able to raise happier and more cooperative youngsters in your blended family. It helps when you know the problems, when to act, and what to do or not to do. The key objective is to be at peace with your role in the stepfamily. The ideal of a nicely functioning stepfamily may never be met. But believing that you have fulfilled your part as God would have you do relieves great stress. Relief is usually found when you realize that you can't always control other people—especially stepchildren.

People in stepfamilies know it is hard work. Some are making it; it can be done. Perhaps the greatest wisdom is in knowing that you can do only so much. What makes a stepfamily work successfully is the dynamics that goes on among all family members. Realizing that you alone cannot be the savior of the whole family will help you to relax and have a more wholesome attitude about your limited role in the stepfamily. When you and your spouse can comfortably back off and not force relationships, the home environment will become much more relaxed as well. One of the finest things a parent can do for a stepchild is to let the child set the pace as far as the emotional development of the relationship is concerned.

No, stepfamilies aren't easy. Many stepparents would like to turn in their buttons. Making stepfamilies work is no bed of roses, but it can be livable.

We might add, too, that much of our counseling ministry is with Christian families, and they have no inside track to immediate success either. Even dedicated Christian parents can and do experience burnout due to their unmet high expectations or ignorance surrounding the real conflicts that go on beneath the surface in family members.

One advantage for the Christian, however, is that he can lean upon the promises of Scripture as well as utilize the power and scope of unconditional love toward family members—as God loves him. In this way stepparents, especially, can take their cues from the Lord. As God loves man not by forcing His way upon us but by being available when needed, so the stepparent can love in the same manner. This kind of love is wanting the very best for an individual—not some sentimental, gushy emotional feeling. Some stepparents we've worked with feel terribly guilty because they don't have a strong rush of feeling for a child. It may be hard for them to hug, kiss, or be tender. This does not mean that they don't, or can't, have the child's best interest at heart. And, remember, wishing for someone's best interest is a form of love too.

As we noted when discussing myths, instant love seldom happens. This may be especially so in stepfamilies because defenses are often very high—both in your children and you. Most stepparents we've worked with have a very strong desire to love and care for the children. But their wanting to be close is blocked by the children who want to hold them off. Here's some excellent advice offered by two different stepmothers:

> If I had a friend who was marrying a man with children, I'd advise her to try to give them a lot of love but not to expect that love to be returned as if she were a real parent.

> The thing you have to learn is not to push yourself on the children. Don't go overboard or be overanxious. Just go along and play it cool. Let them come to you. Accept whatever kind of relationship they want to establish. Be a friend or a mother, whatever they want from you. Don't say, "I want to be a mother to you."

It's hard to "work up" emotional love for any person. What stepparent hasn't at one time or another thought, "Who could ever love this child?" That's OK. It's a normal feeling. Give emotional love time to happen, but don't force it. Learn to exercise patience and you will be greatly rewarded.

You may never "feel" love for your stepchildren, but do not feel guilty over this. You can't always love them as your own. They didn't emotionally bond to you as infants. Many Christians deny some of their emotions. They may label them as bad. To be a "together person" you have to identify and accept yourself if certain expected feelings won't come. You are human . . . you're not sprouting wings yet. And, God does understand if you can't "work up" some feelings. Deal with your negative feelings, and your stepchildren will be the better for it, too. If the feelings of love don't come, work on building your own self-esteem, and it will surprise you how much better the home atmosphere becomes.

One stepmother said to us that some of the best advice she ever received was in a book about stepfamilies. She told us how she had given and given in her home only to be greeted daily by a cold and aloof stepson. She kept thinking that somehow their relationship would right itself. She thought, *He must be as upset over this problem as I am.*

She read the stepfamily book on one of her low days. Such days she called "my ash-heap days." She read about being careful in giving too much of herself, which might lead to burnout, and about how a stepparent must leave room and time for herself. The author went on to state that "one of these days the stepchild will leave and go on his merry little way to start out a new life. The stepparent will be left behind with most of the scars. The stepchild will leave, often giving little thought to the problems of the stepparent who is left behind."

Those words jumped out of the page. She finally realized that her stepson never wanted a real, strong relationship. She accepted that and tried to relate to the stepson as best she could as she reared the other children in the family. She also sought new ways to find fulfillment outside the home. This approach to the problem saved her great heartache.

By taking more care of yourself, you will not be bitter when your stepchild goes to live his own life. The stepparent will then be in a better position to minister where he or she is truly wanted. Then you can better find personal stability as well as make your own home more tension free.

Children need stability as much as they need love. Maybe that's all you can give for the moment, especially if they don't accept you. But what's wrong with providing security? This is *agape* love. A child's life may be disrupted by the breakup of a home. When that happens, he needs to know that his needs will be taken care of and that he can go on and make the best of life with your help.

Agape love is the most powerful influence in the world. If you're devoid of actual feeling but have this form of love for your children, praise God! Without agape love, life has less meaning. This unconditional love, loves not "if" or "when" (based on performance) but "because." The Bible tells us that such love is greater than hope or faith (1 Corinthians 13).

In stepfamilies such consistent caring is vital. Biblically, all parents who have the responsibility of caring for children must have this kind of love. Then parents will realize that children are not possessions to be used or discarded. Christian stepparents, too, must affirm that the children committed to their care are valuable souls for whom Christ died. When you help to provide an affirming, supportive atmosphere, your children will be nurtured. The resultant positive and trusting relationships in the home will immeasurably help the child to develop and mature. The power of true love is set forth in the Bible: "Hatred stirs up strife, but love covers all transgressions" (Proverbs 10:12).

That means that real love can help to overcome almost any obstacle. Most stepchildren will respond in some way when they sense a genuine reaching out to them. Families that have evidenced some measure of success have only arrived there because they have manifested a great amount of caring for the best interests of one another.

Bear in mind that children have a great survival instinct—it is called "the drive for the preservation of life." In most cases when the going gets tough, they will cooperate as they sense deep honesty and openness by adults. On the other hand, they have no trouble spotting phoney or manipulating adults. They know when they are being discounted as persons.

But loving is not always the whole answer. Many times it will not be accepted. Then, everyone in the stepfamily may need help. Don't be too proud to seek it. It does not really matter how much you may know or have experienced in another family setting. It is not a matter of academic training or reading books, as important as these may be.

You are dealing with emotions—raw and intense ones—yours and other people's. That's why we have reiterated numerous times that a third party, in counseling, may be better equipped to get at the underlying attitudes and feelings that need to be explored and expressed. Beware, however, if a counselor attempts to get you to pattern your stepfamily after the natural or biological family in every respect. Such guidance can make things worse.

Christian families can take comfort in the fact that the Bible encourages counseling. Note the following passages:

Where there is no guidance, the people fall, But in abundance of counselors there is victory (Proverbs 11:14).

The way of a fool is right in his own eyes, But a wise man is he who listens to counsel (Proverbs 12:15).

Without consultation, plans are frustrated, But with many counselors they succeed (Proverbs 15:22).

The key, however, if your orientation is Christian, is to be sure to find a counselor who not only understands stepfamily problems but shares your basic value system.

It is our contention that every stepfamily can be successful to some degree. How successful you are will depend upon several key things that we've spelled out. Let's reiterate:

First, success will depend on how hard you try to understand the forces working in your stepchild and yourself. How willing are you to make the effort to combat those forces? Also bear in mind that, although unfortunate, it's true that in no stepfamily are things exactly like the natural biological family.

We have come to see in our own lives and in some families we counsel that an original family can be such a mess that a stepfamily can actually be an improvement if all will work at it!

Let's face it, some stepparents are far better equipped to raise a child than his own parent of the same sex. Parents who are immature, noncaring, selfish, irresponsible, and insecure seldom produce a child who will become a warm, loving, and well-adjusted adult. In many cases we've seen that a stepparent who "has it together" is able to do far more for the child. This can give hope amidst despair and light where darkness seems to abound.

Second, realize that, all in all, there are few neat, quick answers. Keep in front of you the main task as in all parenting: to prepare children for life. Since this involves a process, instant success is pure fantasy. You are dealing with years of conditioning that make it more difficult. If you look for immediate success, you might be setting yourself up for failure.

Third, positive reinforcement is never a maybe in a stepfamily. It is an absolute must. Such reinforcement and support will eventually lead your children toward independence. Rigidly overprotecting and binding them with multiple rules, however, won't adequately prepare them to face the realities of life.

Rejection is the culprit when it comes to the most intense emotion in the family. Children who feel it on a daily basis will react with bad behavior, acting out, and sullenness. This works both ways, too, because children must realize that parents also have their own set of hurts and struggles.

Fourth, you can have a more successful stepfamily if you help your children effectively use coping mechanisms to counter nonproductive defense mechanisms, as outlined in this book. Start by learning to recognize these coping tools and teach your children by example as well as words more appropriate ways of dealing with the stress and anxiety they are experiencing.

Fifth, you must allow free expression by your children of not only surface negative or positive feelings but deeper emotions as well. Ask for help when needed. Adults in stepfamilies also use defenses, and they may need to identify them by seeking support groups or an individual counselor.

Sixth, remove the payoffs for inappropriate behavior in your children by practicing discipline. And, by all means provide rewards for more appropriate behavior. If the child is blocked or has difficulty accepting rewards, positive responses, and compliments for his good behavior, it is a good idea to make him aware of this.

Seventh, as stepparents you must not assume a rescuer's role. Then you won't expect more than what you might receive if the family doesn't totally meet your expectations. This is particularly true for women who have a natural mothering or rescuing quality about them. When a child is hurt, such a woman will deeply feel kindness, sympathy, and protectiveness. But the very deep emotions she feels could be her downfall. It's one thing to provide security for a child but quite another to think of one's self as that child's savior.

Eighth, remember that time can work on your side if you are a stepparent. No deep relationship on earth is without its ups and downs, bumps, misunderstandings, and hardships. A year or two of living together in the stepfamily can build mutuality and at least enough respect for one another to offer reasonable fulfillment.

Ninth, to be successful stepfamilies have to be a cooperative effort. This means that more than the stepparent and children have to be involved. The natural, custodial parent is a vital link, too. His or her main task is to back up the spouse who is the stepparent. This person has to let the children know repeatedly that the stepparent has authority. If this does not happen because the natural parent feels guilty or has the emotional need to protect his children, the family is doomed to catastrophic discord in nearly every case. One parent or child is not totally responsible for the success or failure of the family. An individual parent or child who will not blend or even be reached can, however, negatively affect the whole family.

Tenth, God promises rewards to those who rely upon His promises. Rearing stepfamilies may be one of the hardest tasks in the world, but there are rewards, believe it or not. Sadness and hurt may come your way but to some measure they may be turned to happiness and personal growth. Remember that in whatever manner you have conducted yourself in the stepfamily in the past, this represented the best you could do at the time. Be humble and be able to admit to mistakes and failure. Then pick yourself up and go on. King Solomon said, "He is on the path of life who heeds instruction, but he who forsakes reproof goes astray" (Proverbs 10:17).

Bear in mind that you don't have to go it alone, to depend solely upon human resources. The Lord stands ready to assist if you call upon Him: "In the fear of the Lord there is strong confidence, and his children will have refuge" (Proverbs 14:26).

This means that even in the difficult world of the stepfamily there is refuge, and it can provide you with a service of fulfillment far beyond comprehension. Although it may be tough going, it does not mean that rearing such a family is impossible on every front. It can provide you with the means to rebuild your own life from ashes by giving yourself away to those who may desperately need your love and caring concern. Rewards? Yes, and many. But if you want quick ones, you're setting yourself up to be hurt.

We strongly believe that there are rewards for those who do make the effort to care for another's children. When we became stepparents, we joined a growing host of people who seem to have been given little credit. Each new year over a half million more people fall into this category. Vastly neglected and unrecognized by our society, they need to be seen in most cases as real heroes and heroines, for they have taken on a most difficult task.

Mother's Day and Father's Day have become significant days of the year in America. It is right that we have this recognition for them. But how about a Stepparent's Day? Who has the courage and vision to give dignity to these people who have an unusually difficult role? The time of the year for celebration is immaterial, but let's propose the third or fourth Sunday after Labor Day.

As far as we know, the first church in America to celebrate this day was the First Evangelical Free Church of Orange, California, where the Reverend Mike Fisher is the senior pastor. On September 19, 1982, special recognition was given to the stepparents in the church family during the Sunday services. We would like to challenge the churches of America to begin this kind of recognition. We believe very strongly that a Stepparent's Day is in order and should be initiated by the Christian church for the following reasons:

1. Since both Father's Day and Mother's Day originated in the Christian church, it would be most fitting for a Stepparent's Day to begin in the local church. (See our suggested litany in the appendix.)

2. Of all institutions on earth, the Church ought to be the most caring because on principle the people who should be the most redemptive are those who best understand the meaning of the Cross of Christ.

3. The neighborhood church that celebrates Stepparent's Day builds a bridge of friendship and acceptance to families who need support and love but have not been sure that their participation is welcome.

4. A special day would give dignity, praise, and worthy recognition to a growing host of individuals in our churches and society who rightly should be honored for their great sacrifices and ministry of caring.

5. A Stepparent's Day would better allow stepchildren a special opportunity to express appreciation without feeling uncomfortable over a divided loyalty between a stepparent and the absent, natural parent.

6. A stepparent may not be thanked by a stepchild for years, if ever, for his parenting. A special day might encourage appreciation.

We strongly believe that such a day of recognition is in order. Aristotle once said, "Those who educate children well are more to be honored than those who produce them." He probably did not have stepparents in mind, but this thought could well apply to them. Stepparents are in a position to teach and show by example what marriage can be like and to abolish the biased myths that pervade the thinking about the stepfamily in our society.

Judaism, as well as Christianity, teaches that man must promote the means whereby a human being can develop and mature. The Talmud teaches: "Anyone who brings his friend close to the words of the Torah (wisdom and law), it is as if he had created him." The words of the Torah stress the idea that education is paramount, and that if you teach children as if they were your own, you are as their parent. This is truly an ideal in which a stepparent can rejoice.

In the Bible there are these gracious promises, which can provide encouragement for the stepfamily.

A man will be satisfied with good by the fruit of his words, And the deeds of a man's hands will return to him (Proverbs 12:14).

Cast your bread on the surface of the waters, for you will find it after many days (Ecclesiastes 11:1).

Whatever you do, do your work heartily, as for the Lord rather than for men; knowing that from the Lord you will receive the reward of the inheritance. It is the Lord Christ whom you serve (Colossians 3:23–24).

The Lord is able to grant the strength and wisdom you will need to encounter the unique problems in your stepfamily. He has in our home. We believe in the power of the living Christ to sustain when it gets difficult. He said, "My grace is sufficient for you . . ." (2 Corinthians 12:9).

Biblical promises are especially comforting and positive. Rearing families is the greatest challenge on earth. Isaiah, the Jewish prophet, said, "The work of righteousness will be peace, and the service of righteousness, quietness and confidence forever (Isaiah 32:17).

By relying upon the Lord your life and home can be fulfilling, for the Bible says:

> By wisdom a house is built,
> And by understanding it is established;
> And by knowledge the rooms are filled
> With all precious and pleasant riches.
>   Proverbs 24:3–4

Appendix

Suggested Litany for Stepparent's Day

Minister: Recognizing that no human institution is perfect, will you not expect that perfection in your spouse and stepchildren that belongs only unto the Lord?

Response: Lord, be gracious unto me and help me to so live.

Minister: Realizing that the stepfamily in many ways cannot be like a natural family, will you try not to make it so?

Response: So may it be with the Lord's help.

Minister: Knowing of the special needs of people in a stepfamily, will you allow the individuals freedom of expression?

Response: With God helping me, I will endeavor to so live.

Minister: Recognizing that your ministry is much like that of the Kinsman Redeemer in Old Testament times who voluntarily gave himself to care for those in the family who had special needs and problems, will you continue to try to bring healing for those in your family?

Response: God being my help, I will do so with the best of my ability.

Minister: Realizing your unique service to your family, will you re-
              frain from ever considering yourself as totally replacing
              your stepchildren's natural parent?

Response: So may it be with God's help.

Minister: Knowing the arduous task of helping to raise someone
              else's family, will you practice patience in the face of
              difficulty?

Response: Lord, be gracious unto me and help me to so live.

Minister: Understanding the power of love, will you not attempt to
              force relationships but let them naturally grow closer, and
              when you feel rejected, will you not overreact but look to
              Jesus who was himself despised and rejected of men, yet
              He loved His own?

Response: O God, as I consider your great love for me, so let me begin
              to love my family.

Minister: Considering that you may never be completely accepted by
              your stepchildren, will you accept your role as a ministry in
              and of itself as unto the Lord?

Response: Grant unto me, O Lord, the strength to carry on.

Minister: Realizing your position of authority before the Lord and
              your family, will you enhance the spiritual development of
              your family members, leading an exemplary life before
              them in a Christlike manner?

Response: With the Lord being my help, I will endeavor to give my-
              self wholly to this task.

Prayer

Almighty God, by whom the worlds were made and from whom there
is no hidden thing, we acknowledge Your love and care for a hurting
world. Above the noise and business of life may these folk seek Your
voice and will. We are grateful today for these valiant men and women
who have taken upon themselves a task of love. We thank You for
these so honored today who give of themselves sacrificially. We pray,
Lord, for them, their special hurts and pain. And, though at times

they may feel the sharp pain of rejection, may these stepparents have the special courage to carry on. Give to them the understanding, the caring concern, and patience required to make their lives fulfilled. Help each one to remain faithful to You knowing that You are able to help them meet any challenge. May they listen to You—Your wisdom, Your presence, and Your power. As You have forgiven, may they forgive. As Your grace keeps on giving, may they give. And, may they have the vision today to realize that Your strength is made perfect in their weakness. Today, give them a renewed spirit of steadfast hope and trust when they feel helpless; knowing the promise from Your Word that says: "Be ye steadfast, unmovable, always abounding in the work of the Lord for ye know that your labors are not in vain in the Lord." Give to each the experience of great success and healing in their lives and family. May the faith that makes the heart faithful, and hope that endures, and the love that triumphs over all be with you always, through Jesus Christ our Lord. Amen.

Source Notes

Chapter 1

1. June and William Noble, *How to Live With Other People's Children* (New York: Hawthorn Books, 1977), pp. 2, 3.
2. Brenda Maddox, *The Half-Parent* (New York: New American Library, 1975), p. 29.
3. John and Emily Visher, *Stepfamilies: A Guide to Working With Stepparents and Stepchildren* (New York: Brunner/Mazel Inc., 1979), p. 216.
4. Ibid., pp. 224, 253.
5. Virginia Satir, *Peoplemaking* (Palo Alto, Calif.: Science and Behavior Books, Inc., 1972), pp. 10, 11.
6. Margaret Mead, "Anomalies in American Postdivorce Relationship," in *Divorce and After,* Paul Bohannan, ed. (Garden City, N.Y.: Doubleday & Co., 1970), pp. 107–15.

Chapter 2

1. *The Psychiatric Dictionary,* Leland E. Hinsie, Robert J. Campbell, eds. (New York: Oxford University Press, 1970), p. 180.
2. Otto Fenichel, *The Psychoanalytic Theory of Neurosis* (New York: W. W. Norton & Co., 1945), p. 453.
3. Ruth Roosevelt and Jeannette Lofas, *Living in Step* (New York: McGraw-Hill Book Co., 1976), p. 101.
4. Ibid., p. 111.
5. Richard Gardner, *The Parents Book About Divorce* (Garden City, N.Y.: Doubleday & Co., 1977), p. 204.

Chapter 3

1. Ted W. Engstrom and David J. Juroe, *The Work Trap* (Old Tappan, N.J.: Fleming H. Revell Company, 1979), p. 125.

2. Ibid.
3. Jean and Veryl Rosenbaum, *Stepparenting* (New York: E. P. Dutton, 1978), p. 77.
4. Helen Thomson, *The Successful Stepparent* (New York: Harper & Row, Pubs., Inc., 1966), p. 8.
5. Frederick Capaldi and Barbara McRae, *Stepfamilies: A Cooperative Responsibility* (New York: Franklin Watts, Inc., 1979), pp. 131–35.

Chapter 4

1. Richard Gardner, *The Parents Book About Divorce* (Garden City, N.Y.: Doubleday & Co., 1977), p. 200.
2. Virginia Satir, *Peoplemaking* (Palo Alto, Calif.: Science and Behavior Books, Inc., 1972), p. 181.

Chapter 6

1. Frederick Capaldi and Barbara McRae, *Stepfamilies: A Cooperative Responsibility* (New York: Franklin Watts, Inc., 1979), p. 85.

Chapter 7

1. Richard Gardner, *The Parents Book About Divorce* (Garden City, N.Y.: Doubleday & Co., 1977), p. 106.
2. Jean and Veryl Rosenbaum, *Stepparenting* (New York: E. P. Dutton, 1978), p. 100.
3. Ibid., p. 101.
4. June and William Noble, *How to Live With Other People's Children* (New York: Hawthorn Books, 1977), p. 193.
5. Rosenbaum, op. cit., p. 106.

Chapter 8

1. Leslie Aldridge Westoff, *The Second Time Around* (New York: Viking Press, 1977), p. 90.
2. June and William Noble, *How to Live With Other People's Children* (New York: Hawthorn Books, 1977), p. 76.
3. Ibid., p. 21.

Chapter 9

1. Anne W. Simon, *Stepchild in the Family* (New York: Odyssey Press, 1964), p. 153.
2. Helen Thomson, *The Successful Stepparent* (New York: Harper & Row Pubs., Inc., 1966), p. 46.
3. Richard A. Gardner, *The Parents Book About Divorce* (Garden City, N.Y.: Doubleday & Co., 1977), pp. 230, 231.

Chapter 11

1. Judith S. Wallerstein & Joan B. Kelly, *Surviving the Breakup* (New York: Basic Books, Inc., 1980), p. 54.
2. Helen Thomson, *The Successful Stepparent* (New York: Harper & Row, Pubs., Inc., 1966), pp. 212, 213.

Suggested Reading

Balper, Miriam. *Co-Parenting.* Philadelphia: Running Press, 1978.

Berman, Claire. *Making It As a Stepparent.* Garden City, N.Y.: Doubleday & Co., 1980.

Bohannan, Paul. *Divorce and After.* Garden City, N.Y.: Doubleday & Co., 1971.

Booher, Dianna D. *Coping When Your Family Falls Apart.* New York: Julian Messner, 1979.

Capaldi, Frederick, and McRae, Barbara. *Stepfamilies: A Cooperative Responsibility.* New York: Franklin Watts, Inc., 1979.

Duberman, Lucile. *The Reconstituted Family.* Chicago: Nelson-Hill, Inc., 1975.

Flach, Frederick F. *A New Marriage, a New Life.* New York: McGraw-Hill Book Co., 1978.

Gardner, Richard. *The Parents Book About Divorce.* Garden City, N.Y.: Doubleday & Co., 1977.

Hunt, Morton and Bernice. *The Divorce Experience.* New York: New American Library, 1979.

Maddox, Brenda. *The Half-Parent.* New York: New American Library, 1975.

Noble, June and William. *How to Live With Other People's Children.* New York: Hawthorn Books, 1977.

Reed, Bobby. *Stepfamilies: Living in Christian Harmony.* St. Louis: Concordia Publishing House, 1980.

Roosevelt, Ruth, and Lofas, Jeanette. *Living in Step.* New York: McGraw-Hill Book Co., 1976.

Rosenbaum, Jean and Veryl. *Stepparenting*. New York: E. P. Dutton, 1978.

Satir, Virginia. *Peoplemaking*. Palo Alto, Calif.: Science & Behavior Books, Inc., 1972.

Sheresky, Norman, and Mannes, Marya. *Uncoupling*. New York: Viking Press, 1972.

Simon, Anne W. *Stepchild in the Family*. New York: Odyssey Press, 1964.

Thomson, Helen. *The Successful Stepparent*. New York: Harper & Row, Pubs., Inc., 1966.

Vigeveno, H. S., and Claire, Anne. *Divorce and the Children*. Ventura, Calif.: Regal Books, 1979.

Visher, John and Emily. *Stepfamilies: A Guide to Working with Stepparents and Stepchildren*. New York: Brunner/Mazel, Inc., 1979.

Wallerstein, Judith S., and Kelly, Joan B. *Surviving the Breakup*. New York: Basic Books, Inc., 1980.

Willis, Irene, and Richards, Arlene. *How to Get It Together When Your Parents Are Coming Apart*. New York: David McKay Co., Inc., 1976.

Index